# GRUBBY®
# RECIPES

# GRUBBY®

# RECIPES

# Contents

# ONE:

# PREP

8

# Getting Grubby

# Anyone who says going plant-based means missing meat is telling porkies.

## Satisfaction, not sacrifice

Let's face it, vegan food often gets a bad rap. Too many people think going plant-based means giving up some of life's pleasures. Grubby was founded to prove this is a load of rubbish.

Forget about sloppy ready-meals and ordering another takeaway. The joy and satisfaction of cooking food from scratch is where it's at.

But if you've spent decades using meat and dairy as core ingredients, you need a bit of culinary know-how to avoid munching on rabbit food. That's where we come in...

Grubby is the UK's first fully plant-based recipe kit brand. We've collated 60 of our most popular recipes, packed with flavour, tips and tricks. They're delicious and varied, inspired by cuisines around the world, and only take around 30 minutes to cook. And if that wasn't enough to convince you, each of our recipes contains six varieties of fresh veg, on average. So that's your five a day sorted.

We've split the dishes into three categories, ready for whatever mood you're in. So roll up your sleeves, and get Grubby. The only thing that'll taste like cardboard is the book.

Right: A happy Grubby customer reusing their recipe box.

# The back story

Founded in London back in 2019, our mission has always been to make plant-based eating simple and delicious, so that meat and dairy will never be missed.

In our day to day business we deliver all the pre-portioned ingredients people need to whip up delicious, healthy meals at home, along with easy-to-follow recipe cards and prep playlists to chop along to (look us up on Spotify!).

# Our food philosophy

If everyone ate more plants, the world would be in better shape. From day dot, we've set out to make plants taste so delicious that more people eat them. Whether they're a vegan, a meathead, or anything in between. No judgement here.

We believe food is one of the greatest joys in life. Cooking needn't be tedious. And eating well can be just as fun as eating junk.

## Plants, front and centre

We let the veg do the talking. While meat alternatives have their place, we focus on the incredible flavours and tastes you can get from ingredients grown in the ground.

## Proper portions

A standard line we hear from people trying plant-based is that it doesn't fill them up. Not with our recipes. We never skimp on portion sizes.

## Great ingredients = great food

The quality of the ingredients you put into a dish is as important as the cooking process itself. Using in-season veg makes food fresher, tastier and more nutritious.

## Less is more

We keep ingredient lists short so you don't have to traipse around a busy supermarket or end up on a wild goose chase looking for obscure ingredients.

## Food is medicine

Our recipes are packed with plant points, protein and fibre. All the good stuff necessary for a healthy and strong immune system.

## A recipe for well-being

Cooking good food is an act of love for yourself and anyone you're cooking for. It makes you step back, tune out from the noise of day-to-day life, put your phone down, and focus on what you're creating.

Above: Children at the charity 1moreChild in Jinja, Uganda, enjoying class time.

Right: One of our first local suppliers in Kent out in a cavolo nero field.

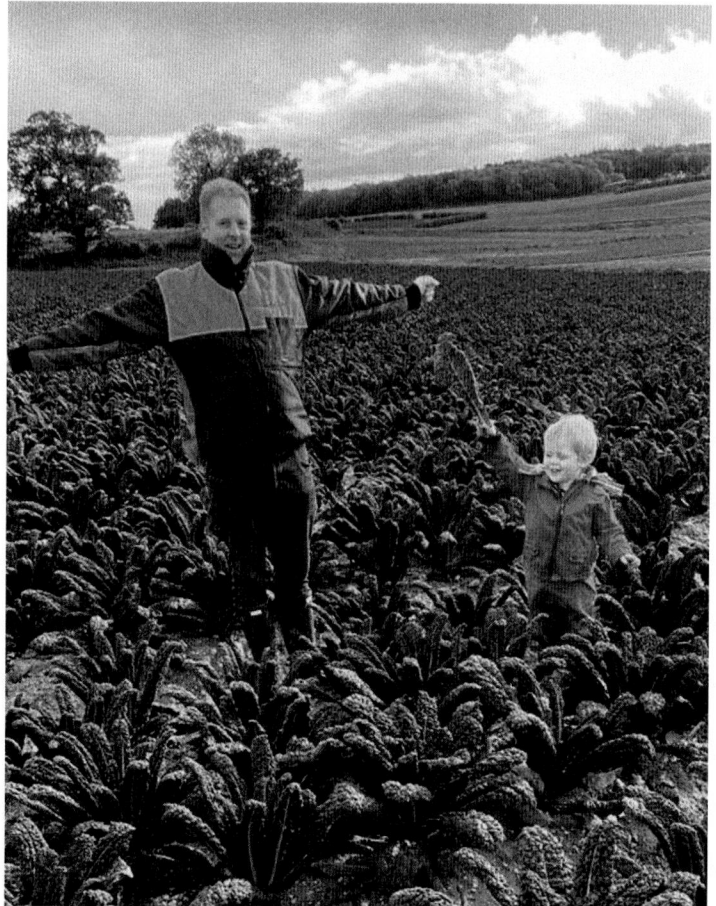

# Doing our bit

We support and partner with family-run farms to bring our customers the best seasonal produce on offer.

We believe no one should go hungry. So for every Grubby box sold, we donate a meal to a child living in poverty through 1morechild.org. So far, we've delivered over 250,000 meals to children in Uganda.

We're also a certified B-Corp, a designation given to companies that meet the highest standards of social and environmental practice. No funny business going on here.

# Taking stock

# Cupboard-based champs that'll have you ready for just about anything.

# Key ingredients

## Olive oil

Regular olive oil can be super versatile and used across heating, salads and dressings. Reserve extra virgin olive oil and it's more robust flavour for finishing dishes. It's made for eating, not heating.

## Sea salt flakes

A non-negotiable in our book. Used by all the top chefs for good reason. Do yourself a favour and stock up on this stuff. It makes a huge difference to the taste of your food.

## Soy sauce

A seasoning power-hitter. Adds depth and complexity to the flavour of a dish without masking the key ingredients. Its salty, tart, savoury flavour can amp up so many dishes, from stews, to creamy pasta sauces to stir-fries and dressings.

## Nuts and seeds

Texture is so important in vegan cooking. Toasting nuts and seeds adds a nutty, crunchy layer to dishes while packing in protein and fibre for added nutrition.

## Miso paste

The secret weapon for those unami, savoury hits. Don't typecast this ingredient for only Japanese dishes. In small quantities, it works well in all sorts from sauces to stews and dressings.

## Henderson's Relish

The vegan equivalent of Worcestershire sauce and a whole lot easier to pronounce. This stuff packs serious flavour. Think of it as a cousin to soy sauce with its own distinctive kick. Perfect for adding extra savoury notes.

## Cashews

For the cheese-toting, egg-flipping non-vegans—parboiled and blended cashews combined with some other ingredients listed on this page are a multi-purpose workhorse for a host of incredible creamy sauces.

## Sesame oil

There's no substitute for its nutty, rich flavour—ideal with noodles, rice, in marinades and sauces, or providing a fragrant element to broths.

## Nutritional yeast

AKA "nooch". This is a cheesy, savoury, B12-rich staple of ours. Super versatile; it has the ability to enhance flavour and nutrition with minimal effort. Perfect for pasta, sauces, toppings and more.

## Rose harissa

This isn't as hot as normal harissa and gives more of a fragrant, slow-burning chilli heat, perfect for all kinds of dishes. It adds depth and spice to roasted veg and can also be stirred through coconut yoghurt as an accompaniment or marinade.

## Cornflour

Cornflour isn't just for thickening sauces; it's the secret to getting those ASMR-worthy crispy finishes. Perfect for oyster mushrooms and tofu chunks, once you start using it in your frying process, you'll be hooked.

## Peanut butter

Great on toast (obvs), but there's more to it than that. We love it in curries, stir-fries and lots of amazing cold dressings too.

## Agave syrup

We use this a lot. It's a honey replacement that brings a natural sweetness to stews, tagines and any sauce where you need a sweet note.

## Dijon mustard

Brings a different type of peppery heat to sauces and dressings. Works well in creamy sauces and vinaigrettes.

## White wine vinegar

If in doubt, add a little acid. Subtly sweet and full of tang. White wine vinegar adds serious zip to dressings and in small doses can lift sauces.

## Rice vinegar

Made from fermented rice, it's lighter in colour and flavour than wine vinegars. Perfect in slaws and dressings.

## Tahini

Great with all Middle Eastern dishes. The creamy sesame seed paste is a genius addition to just about anything, from classic hummus to an assortment of our house blends.

## Sriracha

For those who like stuff hot, this is a must. It's great as part of a sticky coating and can take your stir-fries to the next level.

## Tomato purée

This'll give you that deep tomato flavour you can't easily get from fresh tomatoes. Works in all kinds of stews and curries and when making your own curry paste. Always best added early on to one-pot dishes when the onions and garlic have softened.

## Capers

Not everyone's cup of tea on their own, but they're great for salty bursts of flavour in tomato-based pasta sauces or blended into pesto.

# Equipment

Sharp knife
Knife sharpener
Chopping board
Colander and sieve
Selection of bowls
Oven trays
Selection of pots and lids
Non-stick frying pan
Large deep-sided frying pan
Grater
Peeler
Spatulas
Whisk
Measuring jug
Measuring spoons
Scales
Blender
Garlic crusher
Tongs
Ovenproof dishes

# Covering bases

# These killer concoctions will add a shed load of flavour without a shed load of effort.

## Satay sauce

| | |
|---|---|
| 1 clove | Garlic |
| 30g | Ginger |
| 2 tbsp | Tamari |
| 1 | Red chilli |
| 1 tbsp | Agave syrup |
| 1 tbsp | White wine vinegar |
| 3 tbsp | Peanut butter |

Press the garlic, finely chop the chilli
and combine all the ingredients in a small
bowl and stir well. Perfect in stir-fries or
over roasted aubergine.

## Green cashew pesto

| | |
|---|---|
| 30g | Cashews |
| Handful | Basil |
| 1 | Lemon, juiced |
| 1 tbsp | Nutritional yeast |
| 1 clove | Garlic |
| 4 tbsp | Olive oil |
| Pinch | Salt |
| Pinch | Pepper |

Blend all the ingredients together
until you have a rough pesto. Also
works nicely with hazelnuts in place
of the cashews. Great through
traybakes and pastas.

## Miso coating

| | |
|---|---|
| 30g | Ginger |
| 2 tbsp | Miso paste |
| 1 tbsp | Soy sauce |
| 1 | Lime, juiced |
| 1 tbsp | Rice vinegar |
| 1 tbsp | Sesame oil |

Peel and grate the ginger and place
into a small bowl along with all the
other ingredients and mix well. This is a
winner slapped over roasted aubergines,
portobello mushrooms, or served with
coconut rice and green veggies.

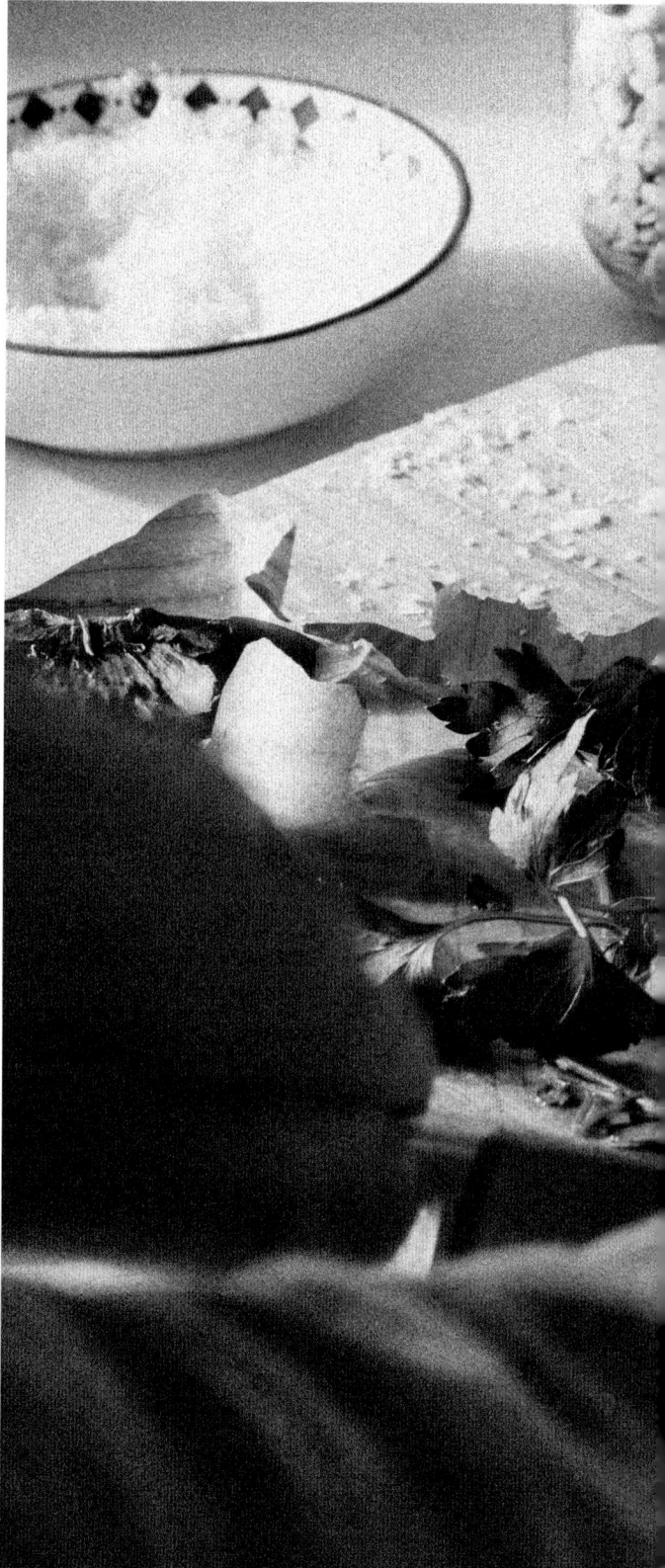

## Cucumber coconut raita

| | |
|---|---|
| 1 | Cucumber |
| 2 tsp | Mint sauce |
| 200ml | Coconut yoghurt |
| 2 tbsp | Olive oil |
| 1 clove | Garlic |
| Pinch | Salt |
| Pinch | Pepper |

Scoop out the seeds from the cucumber and roughly grate. Use a tea towel or kitchen roll to remove excess liquid. Grate the garlic. Then combine all the ingredients in a bowl. Leave to chill until you're ready to serve. Great alongside curries or as a dipping sauce.

## Creamy pasta sauce

| | |
|---|---|
| 60g | Cashews |
| 1 | Vegetable stock cube |
| 1 tbsp | Nutritional yeast |
| 1 tbsp | Soy sauce |
| 200ml | Plant-based cream |
| 2 cloves | Garlic |
| 1 | Lemon, juiced |
| 1 tsp | Dijon mustard |

Parboil the cashews for 5 minutes, then drain. Add to a blender with the remaining ingredients and blitz until smooth. We love this as a carbonara base.

## Cashew 'parmesan' topping

| | |
|---|---|
| 60g | Cashews |
| 2 tbsp | Nutritional yeast |
| ½ tsp | Garlic powder |
| Pinch | Salt |
| Pinch | Pepper |

Simply blitz all the ingredients together until you have a fine crumb. This topping gives a super cheesy salty hit to any dish that deserves it.

## Ragù

| | |
|---|---|
| 1 | Carrot |
| 1 | Onion |
| 2 cloves | Garlic |
| 250g | Chestnut mushrooms |
| 1 tsp | Italian herbs |
| 1 tbsp | Tomato purée |
| 200g | Cooked lentils |
| 1 | Vegetable stock cube |
| 1 tbsp | Tamari |
| 1 tsp | Henderson's Relish |
| 1 tbsp | Onion jam |
| 250ml | Boiling water |

Finely chop the carrot, onion, garlic and mushrooms. Fry in plant-based butter for 5–6 minutes until softening. Add everything else except the water and stir through for a minute to combine. Then add the water and gently simmer for 20 minutes until oozy. Great on all kinds of pastas, or stirred through crispy pan-fried gnocchi.

## Grubby curry paste

| | |
|---|---|
| 30g | Ginger |
| 1 | Lime, juiced |
| 1 tbsp | Rose harissa paste |
| 1 tbsp | Tomato purée |
| 2 tsp | Curry powder |
| 30g | Cashews |
| 1 tbsp | Mango chutney |
| 2 tbsp | Water |

Peel the ginger and roughly cut. Add to a blender with all the other ingredients and blitz until smooth. This really packs a punch and it's well worth the effort. It's a Korma vibe so goes well in any coconut- or tomato-based curries.

## Cashew béchamel sauce

| | |
|---|---|
| 100g | Cashews |
| 300ml | Boiling water |
| 2 tbsp | Nutritional yeast |
| 1 tbsp | Olive oil |
| Pinch | Salt |
| Pinch | Pepper |

Parboil the cashews for 5 minutes, then leave to cool for 10 minutes before adding to a blender with the cooking water. Add the remaining ingredients and blitz until smooth. Ideal for a moussaka, lasagne and any cheesy pasta.

## Hummus

| | |
|---|---|
| 1 tin | Chickpeas |
| 4 tbsp | Tahini |
| 75ml | Olive oil |
| 1 clove | Garlic |
| 1 | Lemon |
| Pinch | Cayenne pepper |
| Pinch | Salt |
| Pinch | Pepper |

Pour a few tablespoons of the chickpea water into the blender. Then drain the rest. Add all the ingredients to the blender and blitz until smooth. Rose harissa paste is always a great addition if you want to spice things up. Za'atar or chermoula are good too.

## Spicy peanut dressing

| | |
|---|---|
| 1 | Lime, juiced |
| 1 tbsp | Sesame oil |
| 1 tbsp | Agave syrup |
| 1 tbsp | Miso paste |
| 2 tbsp | Peanut butter |
| 1 tbsp | Sriracha |

Combine all the ingredients in a bowl and stir well. Great in salads and slaws.

## Green goddess sauce

| | |
|---|---|
| 1 | Avocado |
| Handful | Coriander |
| Handful | Dill |
| 1 clove | Garlic |
| 1 tsp | Capers |
| 1 | Lime |
| 3 tbsp | Water |
| 2 tbsp | Olive oil |
| Pinch | Salt |
| Pinch | Pepper |

Peel and chop the avocado and place into a blender. Add the other ingredients and blend until smooth. You'll use this again and again. A great dip for nachos, it's awesome over salads and also works stirred through pastas.

## Crispy coating

| | |
|---|---|
| 1 tbsp | Soy sauce |
| 1 tbsp | Nutritional yeast |
| Pinch | Salt |
| Pinch | Pepper |
| 50g | Cornflour |

Our favourite crispy coating for tofu or oyster mushrooms. Marinade your chosen ingredient in the soy sauce and nutritional yeast for 10–15 minutes. Drain off any excess liquid and then toss in the cornflour and seasoning. Mix well, then place into hot oil until golden and crispy. You can jazz it up with different herbs, like oregano, cayenne, or even sriracha for extra heat.

# TWO:

COOK

# Comfort food

# Dishes that are like a warm blanket. Just much tastier.

40 mins
Serves 2

# Aubergine, lentil and courgette moussaka topped with creamy cashew béchamel sauce

| | |
|---|---|
| 60g | Cashews |
| 1 | Courgette |
| 1 | Aubergine |
| 1 | Onion |
| 3 | Garlic cloves |
| 400g tin | Lentils |
| 1 tbsp | Tomato purée |
| 400g | Tomato passata |
| 1 tbsp | Henderson's Relish |
| 1 tsp | Dried oregano |
| 1 | Vegetable stock cube |
| 1 tbsp | Nutritional yeast |
| Handful | Rocket |

1 Preheat the oven to 200°C/180°C fan/gas mark 6.

2 Tip the cashews into a bowl, pour over 300ml boiling water and leave to soak. Top, tail and slice the courgette and aubergine lengthways into 5mm slices. Add the courgette and aubergine slices to a baking tray, drizzle with olive oil and season with salt and pepper. Roast in the oven for 15 minutes until soft.

3 Meanwhile, dice the onion and crush the garlic. Heat a drizzle of olive oil in a deep-sided frying pan over a medium heat. Add the onion and a pinch of salt and soften for 3–4 minutes, then add the garlic and cook for 30 seconds more. Add the lentils (no need to drain), along with the tomato purée, tomato passata, Henderson's Relish and oregano. Crumble in the stock cube. Bring to the boil, then simmer over a medium heat for 8–10 minutes until really thick. Season well.

4 Tip the soaked cashews and their soaking liquid into a blender. Add the nutritional yeast, 1 tablespoon of olive oil and a pinch of salt and pepper. Blitz until smooth.

5 Build your moussaka by pouring half of the lentil mixture into an ovenproof dish. Top with half the aubergine and courgette slices, then repeat with the remaining lentil mixture and vegetable slices. Pour the cashew sauce all over the top and spread evenly to cover the filling. Bake for 25–30 minutes.

6 Meanwhile, dress the rocket in a drizzle of olive oil and a pinch of salt and pepper. Serve the moussaka with the rocket on the side.

# Cashew and avocado pesto pasta with griddled courgettes and sun-dried tomatoes

| | |
|---|---|
| 60g | Cashews |
| 1 | Courgette |
| 200g | Rigatoni or penne pasta |
| 1 | Avocado |
| Handful | Basil |
| 1 tbsp | Nutritional yeast |
| 3 | Garlic cloves |
| 1 | Lemon |
| 100g | Sun-dried tomatoes in oil |
| Handful | Rocket |

1 Tip the cashews into a large saucepan of boiling water and simmer for 5 minutes. Meanwhile, slice the courgette into 1cm rounds and set aside for later. Using a slotted spoon, remove the cashews from the saucepan and set aside in a bowl. Bring the pan of water back to the boil, add the pasta, and simmer for 10 minutes.

2 To make the pesto, peel and stone the avocado and add the flesh to a blender, along with the basil, cashew nuts, nutritional yeast, garlic, 2 tablespoons of olive oil and 150ml water. Squeeze in half the lemon and blitz until smooth.

3 Heat a good drizzle of olive oil in a deep-sided frying pan over a high heat. Add the courgette slices and cook for 2–3 minutes on each side until charred, then take off the heat.

4 Once the pasta is cooked, loosely drain and return to the saucepan over a low heat, stirring through the pesto, courgette slices and sun-dried tomatoes. Warm through for 2 minutes.

5 Spoon the pesto pasta into serving bowls and top with a handful of fresh rocket, and a good squeeze of the remaining lemon.

# Butternut squash risotto with crispy kale and toasted pumpkin seeds

| | |
|---|---|
| 1 | Butternut squash, peeled and deseeded |
| 1 tsp | Paprika |
| 1 | Onion |
| 2 | Garlic cloves |
| 1 | Leek |
| 1 tbsp | Nutritional yeast |
| ½ tsp | Ground coriander |
| 150g | Arborio rice |
| 50ml | White wine |
| 1 | Vegetable stock cube |
| 200g | Kale |
| 20g | Pumpkin seeds |

1 Preheat the oven to 200°C/180°C fan/gas mark 6.

2 Chop the butternut squash into 2cm chunks. Toss on a roasting tray with the paprika and 1 tablespoon of olive oil, and roast for 30 minutes.

3 Meanwhile, finely chop the onion and garlic, and thinly slice the leek. Heat 1 tablespoon of olive oil in a deep-sided frying pan over a medium heat. Add the onion and leek and soften for 4–5 minutes, then add the garlic, nutritional yeast, ground coriander, arborio rice and a pinch of salt and pepper. Stir and cook for a further 2 minutes, then add the white wine and cook for 1–2 minutes until absorbed.

4 In a jug, dissolve the stock cube in 800ml boiling water. Gradually add the stock to the pan, about 100ml at a time and letting each addition absorb into the rice, until the rice is cooked through and all the liquid is absorbed. This should take 20–25 minutes.

5 Roughly chop the kale and arrange on a separate roasting tray. Add 1 tablespoon of olive oil and a pinch of salt, and scrunch together for a minute to help soften the kale. Roast for 4–5 minutes until charred and crispy. At the same time, toast the pumpkin seeds in a hot, dry pan for 3 minutes until popping and golden.

6 Once the butternut squash is soft, tip two-thirds of it into a blender, along with 150ml hot water. Blitz until you have a smooth sauce. Stir the butternut purée into the risotto and allow the mixture to thicken for 2–3 minutes. Serve with the remaining butternut chunks, topped with the crispy kale and toasted pumpkin seeds.

20 mins
Serves 2

# Cashew and mushroom spaghetti carbonara with fresh rocket

| | |
|---|---|
| 250g | Chestnut mushrooms |
| 200g | Linguine |
| 60g | Cashews |
| 2 | Garlic cloves |
| 1 tbsp | Nutritional yeast |
| 200ml | Plant-based cream |
| 1 tbsp | Soy sauce |
| 1 | Lemon |
| Handful | Rocket |

1   Chop the mushrooms into quarters. Heat a drizzle of olive oil in a large frying pan over a high heat. Add the mushrooms and a pinch of salt and pepper. Fry for 5–6 minutes until soft and golden.

2   Cook the linguine in a large saucepan of boiling water over a medium heat for 10–12 minutes until cooked through.

3   To make the sauce, soak the cashews in boiling water for 5 minutes. Peel the garlic cloves and add to a blender with the soaked cashews, nutritional yeast, plant-based cream and soy sauce. Squeeze in half the lemon and add a pinch of salt and pepper. Blitz until you have a smooth, creamy consistency. Pour the blended sauce into the frying pan with the mushrooms, and reduce to a low simmer.

4   Loosely drain the linguine, then stir it into the pan with the mushrooms and sauce. Add two-thirds of the rocket and stir to combine. Use tongs to twist the saucy linguine into serving bowls, then top with the remaining rocket and another squeeze of lemon.

# Oven-baked chickpea dahl with chilli-cheese naans

| | |
|---|---|
| 1 | Red onion |
| 2 | Garlic cloves |
| 30g | Fresh ginger |
| 1 | Green chilli |
| 120g | Red split lentils |
| 400g tin | Chickpeas |
| 1 tbsp | Medium curry powder |
| ½ tsp | Ground turmeric |
| 400ml | Coconut milk |
| 1 | Vegetable stock cube |
| 50g | Plant-based cheese |
| 2 | Naan breads |
| 30g | Plant-based butter |
| Handful | Coriander |

1 Preheat the oven to 200°C/180°C fan/gas mark 6.

2 Finely slice the red onion. Peel and finely chop the garlic and ginger. Finely chop the green chilli. Rinse the red lentils in a sieve and set aside, then drain and rinse the chickpeas.

3 Tip half the sliced onion, half the chopped garlic and half the chopped chilli into an ovenproof dish. Next, add the chopped ginger, medium curry powder and turmeric, along with the drained chickpeas and lentils. Pour the coconut milk and 100ml boiling water over the top, crumble in the stock cube, give everything a good stir and cover tightly with foil. Bake for 20 minutes.

4 Meanwhile, finely grate the plant-based cheese. Arrange the naans on a baking tray and spread each with some plant-based butter. Sprinkle over the remaining green chilli and garlic, then top with the plant-based cheese.

5 Once the dahl is almost ready, add the naans to the oven for the final 5 minutes, or until the cheese has melted. Once done, remove the tin foil from the dahl. Give it a really good stir until the lentils break down and everything comes together and thickens. Pick the coriander leaves from their stalks.

6 Serve the dahl in bowls, garnished with the remaining red onion and the coriander leaves. Season with a pinch of pepper and serve the chilli-cheese naans on the side for dipping.

# Creamy miso, coconut and aubergine ramen with udon noodles

| | |
|---|---|
| 1 | Aubergine |
| 4 | Portobello mushrooms |
| 1 | Vegetable stock cube |
| 3 | Spring onions |
| 400ml | Coconut milk |
| 1 tbsp | Soy sauce |
| 1 tbsp | Miso paste |
| 1 tsp | Mirin |
| ½ tsp | Chilli flakes |
| 400g | Udon noodles |
| 1 tbsp | Sesame oil |
| 1 | Lime |
| Handful | Coriander |

1 Preheat the oven to 220°C/200°C fan/gas mark 7.

2 Cut the aubergine into chunks and place them on a baking tray. Drizzle with oil and a pinch of salt, and mix well. Roast for 20–25 minutes, or until the aubergine is soft.

3 Meanwhile, slice the mushrooms. Heat a drizzle of vegetable oil in a large saucepan over a medium heat. Add the mushrooms and a pinch of salt, and fry for 5–6 minutes until soft and golden.

4 Dissolve the stock cube in a jug with 400ml boiling water and finely slice the spring onions. Once the mushrooms are cooked, pour over the stock and add the coconut milk, soy sauce, miso paste, mirin, chilli flakes, and half of the spring onions. Reduce the heat to low and simmer for 10–15 minutes.

5 Meanwhile, place the noodles in a large bowl and pour over enough boiling water to cover. Let them soak for 4–5 minutes before carefully breaking them apart. Drain well and set aside.

6 Once the aubergine is cooked, transfer it to the pan with the broth. Add the noodles and sesame oil, and simmer for another 2–3 minutes. To serve, spoon the broth into bowls and top with the remaining spring onions. Finish with a squeeze of lime juice, and some fresh coriander leaves.

35 mins
Serves 2

# Crispy oyster mushroom burgers with pesto mayo and Parmentier potatoes

| | |
|---|---|
| 2 | Potatoes |
| 3 | Garlic cloves |
| 1 tsp | Dried oregano |
| 250g | Cherry tomatoes |
| 300g | Oyster mushrooms |
| 1 tbsp | Soy sauce |
| 3 tbsp | Cornflour |
| 1 tbsp | Nutritional yeast |
| 2 tbsp | Plant-based mayo |
| 1 tbsp | Plant-based green pesto |
| Handful | Rocket |
| 1 tsp | Balsamic vinegar |
| 2 | Ciabatta rolls |

1 Preheat the oven to 220°C/200°C fan/gas mark 7.

2 Cut the potatoes into small bite-sized pieces and roughly chop the garlic. Combine them on a baking tray, and drizzle with vegetable oil. Sprinkle over the oregano and a pinch of salt and pepper. Roast for 25–30 minutes until golden brown, adding the cherry tomatoes to the tray for the final 10 minutes.

3 Meanwhile, tip the mushrooms into a large bowl (tear any larger ones in half) and pour over the soy sauce. Leave to soak for 2–3 minutes while you heat a generous drizzle of vegetable oil in a large frying pan over a medium–high heat. Once the mushrooms have soaked, add the cornflour and nutritional yeast to the bowl and mix well. Once the oil is hot, carefully add the mushrooms to the pan. Fry for 3–4 minutes on each side until golden brown and crispy. Once cooked, set aside.

4 For the pesto mayo, mix together the mayo, pesto and a pinch of pepper in a small bowl, then set aside. In a separate large bowl, combine the rocket and balsamic vinegar and toss well.

5 Halve the ciabatta rolls and place them in the oven for 2–3 minutes until warmed through and starting to crisp.

6 To serve, spread the base of each roll with the pesto mayo, then stack the crispy mushrooms on top, followed by the oven-roasted tomatoes and some of the rocket. Serve with the crispy potatoes and the remaining rocket and tomatoes.

30 mins
Serves 2

# Curried aubergine and fragrant rice with minty coconut yoghurt and beef tomato

| | |
|---|---|
| 1 | Onion |
| 2 | Garlic cloves |
| 1 tsp | Turmeric |
| 150g | Basmati rice |
| 1 | Aubergine |
| 2 tsp | Mild curry powder |
| 3 tbsp | Coconut yoghurt |
| 1 large | Tomato |
| Handful | Coriander |
| 1 tsp | Mint sauce |
| 2 tbsp | Crispy dried onions |

1   Preheat the oven to 220°C/200°C fan/gas mark 7.

2   Finely dice the onion and garlic. Heat a drizzle of vegetable oil in a saucepan over a medium heat. Add the onion and garlic and fry for 2–3 minutes before adding half the turmeric. Fry for a further minute, then add the rice and 300ml boiling water. Bring to the boil, then reduce the heat to low and simmer for 10–12 minutes until the water has been absorbed.

3   Meanwhile, slice the aubergine into 1cm discs and place in a large bowl. Add the curry powder, the remaining turmeric and 1 tablespoon of the coconut yoghurt and mix well, ensuring that all the aubergine pieces are covered in the spice paste. Arrange in a single layer on a baking tray and place in the oven for 15–17 minutes until cooked through.

4   Meanwhile, finely dice the tomato and tip it into a small bowl. Finely chop the coriander and add half to the tomato (save the rest for later). Season with salt and a drizzle of vegetable oil and set aside. Combine the remaining coconut yoghurt and mint sauce in a separate small bowl.

5   Once the rice is cooked, give it a good stir. Remove the aubergine from the oven and serve on top of the rice. Finish with spoonfuls of tomato and the mint yoghurt, topping with the remaining coriander leaves and the crispy onions.

# Chickpea, apricot and sweet potato tagine with herb and lemon bulgur wheat

| | |
|---|---|
| 1 | Onion |
| 2 | Garlic cloves |
| 40g | Dried apricots |
| 1 tbsp | Tomato purée |
| 1 tbsp | Rose harissa |
| 1 tbsp | Ras el hanout |
| 1 | Sweet potato |
| 400g tin | Chickpeas |
| 2 | Vegetable stock cubes |
| 80g | Bulgur wheat |
| Handful | Mint |
| Handful | Coriander |
| Handful | Pomegranate seeds |
| 1 | Lemon |

1 Finely slice the onion, crush the garlic and chop the apricots. Heat a drizzle of vegetable oil in a large, deep-sided frying pan over a medium heat. Add the onion and fry for 4–5 minutes until softening, then add the garlic and fry for a further minute. Add the apricots, tomato purée, harissa and ras el hanout, and stir well. Reduce the heat to low, stirring occasionally.

2 Peel and chop the sweet potato into 1cm cubes. Drain the chickpeas and add both to the onion pan. Season with a pinch of salt and pepper. Stir to coat the veg in the spices, then increase the heat to medium and continue to fry for 4–5 minutes.

3 Add 500ml boiling water to the pan and crumble in one of the stock cubes. Bring to the boil, then reduce the heat to low and simmer for 20 minutes until the veg are cooked through.

4 Meanwhile, rinse the bulgur wheat in a sieve under cold water, then add it to a saucepan with the remaining stock cube and 180ml boiled water. Cover with the lid and simmer for 15 minutes. Once done, transfer to a large bowl, stir well and set aside to cool.

5 Finely chop the mint and coriander and add to the bowl with the bulgur wheat, along with the pomegranate seeds. Zest the lemon into the bowl and squeeze in half the juice. Mix well. Serve the herby bulgur wheat on plates, then spoon over the tagine and finish with a squeeze of the remaining lemon.

30 mins
Serves 2

# Sicilian aubergine linguine with sun-dried tomatoes, black olives and capers

| | |
|---|---|
| 1 | Aubergine |
| 2 | Garlic cloves |
| 1 | Red onion |
| 1 tsp | Mixed Italian herbs |
| ½ tsp | Chilli flakes |
| 2 tbsp | Sun-dried tomato purée |
| 400g | Tomato passata |
| 40g | Black olives |
| 1 | Vegetable stock cube |
| 200g | Linguine |
| Handful | Parsley |
| Handful | Baby spinach |

1   Preheat the oven to 220°C/200°C fan/gas mark 7.

2   Start by roughly chopping the aubergine into 3cm cubes. Place the cubes on a baking tray and drizzle with olive oil. Season with a pinch of salt and pepper. Roast for 20 minutes, or until soft and slightly charred.

3   Meanwhile, finely dice the garlic and red onion, and roughly chop the olives. Heat a drizzle of olive oil in a large, deep-sided frying pan over a medium heat. Add the garlic and onion and fry for 5–6 minutes, or until soft. Then add the dried Italian herbs, chilli flakes, sun-dried tomato purée, tomato passata and olives. Crumble in the stock cube and add 100ml boiling water. Stir everything together, then reduce the heat to low and let it simmer gently for 10–12 minutes.

4   While the sauce is simmering, cook the linguine in a saucepan of boiling water for 10–12 minutes, or until it is soft with a slight bite. Finely chop the parsley and set aside.

5   Once the aubergine is cooked, remove it from the oven and add it to the tomato sauce, along with the spinach. Stir to combine, then take off the heat and season to taste. If the sauce is too thick at this point, you can add a little more water to adjust the consistency.

6   Drain the linguine and stir it through the pan with the sauce, then serve topped with the finely chopped parsley.

15 mins
Serves 2

# Crispy pan-fried gnocchi bolognese with mushrooms and walnuts

| | |
|---|---|
| 200g | Gnocchi |
| 250g | Chestnut mushrooms |
| 2 | Spring onions |
| 2 | Garlic cloves |
| 1 | Vegetable stock cube |
| 1 tbsp | Tomato purée |
| 1 tbsp | Nutritional yeast |
| 1 tsp | Dried oregano |
| 40g | Walnuts |
| Handful | Basil |
| 1 tbsp | Soy sauce |

1  Heat a drizzle of olive oil in a large, deep-sided frying pan over a medium–high heat. Add the gnocchi and cook for 5 minutes until starting to colour and crisp.

2  Meanwhile, coarsely grate the chestnut mushrooms, and finely slice the spring onions and garlic. Dissolve the stock cube in a jug with 250ml boiling water. Add the tomato purée, nutritional yeast and oregano to the jug and stir.

3  After 5 minutes, add the grated mushrooms to the gnocchi pan, along with the sliced spring onions and garlic. Increase the heat to high and cook for 5 minutes until softened. Meanwhile, finely chop the walnuts and basil.

4  Once the mushrooms are softened, add the soy sauce to the pan and cook for a further minute. Add the tomato stock mixture, chopped walnuts and half of the chopped basil and stir together. Simmer for 1–2 minutes until nicely combined, then season with a generous pinch of pepper.

5  Serve the gnocchi bolognese in bowls, topped with the remaining chopped basil and a pinch of pepper.

15 mins
Serves 2

# Creamy rose harissa and butter bean stew with spinach, cherry tomatoes and fresh basil

| | |
|---|---|
| 2 | Garlic cloves |
| 250g | Cherry tomatoes |
| ½ tsp | Chilli flakes |
| 1 tbsp | Tomato purée |
| 400g tin | Butter beans |
| 1 tbsp | Rose harissa |
| 1 | Vegetable stock cube |
| 2 | Ciabatta rolls |
| Handful | Baby spinach |
| Handful | Basil |
| 2 tbsp | Plant-based mayo |

1. Peel and finely slice the garlic, and halve the cherry tomatoes. Heat a drizzle of olive oil in a large, deep-sided frying pan over a medium heat. Add the garlic, tomatoes and chilli flakes and cook for 2 minutes.

2. Add the tomato purée and cook for 1 minute more, then add the butter beans (no need to drain) and rose harissa. Crumble in the stock cube, stir and bring to the boil, then reduce the heat to low and simmer for 3–4 minutes until thickened.

3. Meanwhile, cut the ciabatta rolls in half and heat them in the toaster until crisp and golden.

4. Add the spinach to the pan and cover with a lid. Cook for 1–2 minutes until the spinach is wilted. Finely chop the basil and add this to the pan, along with the mayo. Stir and season with a pinch of salt and pepper.

5. Serve the stew in bowls with the toasted ciabatta on the side for dipping. Garnish with the remaining basil, a drizzle of olive oil and a pinch of pepper.

# Crispy gnocchi puttanesca with Tenderstem broccoli, roasted red onions and pumpkin seeds

| | |
|---|---|
| 2 | Red onions |
| 2 | Garlic cloves |
| 1 tbsp | Tomato purée |
| 1 tsp | Red wine vinegar |
| 1 tsp | Mixed Italian herbs |
| 400g | Tomato passata |
| 1 | Vegetable stock cube |
| 40g | Black olives |
| 1 tbsp | Capers |
| 1 tbsp | Nutritional yeast |
| 200g | Tenderstem broccoli |
| 250g | Cherry tomatoes |
| 200g | Gnocchi |
| 20g | Pumpkin seeds |

1  Preheat the oven to 220°C/200°C fan/gas mark 7.

2  To make the puttanesca sauce, finely slice one of the onions and the garlic. Heat a drizzle of olive oil in a large, deep-sided frying pan over a medium heat. Add the sliced onion and garlic and fry for 4–5 minutes until starting to soften, then add the tomato purée, red wine vinegar and Italian herbs and cook for a further 1–2 minutes. Pour in the tomato passata and crumble in the stock cube. Bring to the boil, then reduce the heat to low. Roughly chop the olives and capers and add to the pan, along with the nutritional yeast. Simmer for 10–12 minutes until the sauce has thickened. Season to taste with salt and pepper.

3  Meanwhile, cut the remaining onion into wedges and place on a baking tray with the Tenderstem broccoli and cherry tomatoes. Drizzle with olive oil and season with salt and pepper. Roast for 10–12 minutes until starting to colour.

4  Heat 1 tablespoon of olive oil in a separate large frying pan over a high heat. Add the gnocchi and fry for 6–7 minutes until golden brown. At the same time, lightly toast the pumpkin seeds in a small, dry frying pan over a medium heat for 3–4 minutes until popping and slightly charred.

5  Once the sauce is ready, add the gnocchi and mix well. Serve in bowls, topped with the roasted veg and pumpkin seeds.

# Gochujang mac and 'cheese' with crispy sesame tofu

| | |
|---|---|
| 280g | Firm tofu |
| 2 tsp | Gochujang paste |
| 1 tbsp | Soy sauce |
| 2½ tbsp | Cornflour |
| 1 | Red pepper |
| 1 tsp | Sesame seeds |
| 200g | Macaroni |
| 1 | Vegetable stock cube |
| 100g | Plant-based cheese |
| 1 tbsp | Nutritional yeast |
| 250ml | Plant-based cream |
| 2 | Spring onions |

1 Crumble the tofu into small pieces and tip into a large bowl, along with 1 teaspoon of the gochujang paste and the soy sauce. Mix well, then sprinkle over 2 tablespoons of the cornflour and mix again. Set aside.

2 Finely slice the red pepper. Heat a drizzle of vegetable oil in a large frying pan over a high heat. Once hot, add the sliced red pepper to the pan and fry for 4–5 minutes until cooked. Remove from the pan and set aside on a plate.

3 Return the pan to a medium–high heat and add the tofu. Fry for 5 minutes, then add the sesame seeds and continue to cook for 2–3 minutes more until the tofu is golden and crispy.

4 Meanwhile, cook the macaroni in a large saucepan of boiling water for 8–10 minutes until tender.

5 To make the sauce, crumble the stock cube into a small bowl and grate in the plant-based cheese. Add the nutritional yeast and plant-based cream, along with the remaining ½ tablespoon of cornflour and 1 teaspoon of gochujang paste. Stir in 150ml boiling water and season with salt and pepper.

6 Once the macaroni is cooked, loosely drain and return it to the saucepan. Pour over the sauce and cook over a low heat until the sauce has thickened slightly. Add the cooked pepper to the pan and stir through. Finely slice the spring onions.

7 Serve the macaroni in bowls, topped with the crispy tofu and spring onion slices.

# Mushroom gyros with cucumber raita, Greek salad and oregano fries

| | |
|---|---|
| 2 | Large potatoes |
| 2 tsp | Dried oregano |
| 4 | Portobello mushrooms |
| 3 | Garlic cloves |
| 1 tsp | Paprika |
| 1 tsp | Ground cumin |
| 1 | Cucumber |
| 2 tbsp | Coconut yoghurt |
| 1 | Lemon |
| 1 | Red onion |
| 1 | Tomato |
| 4 | Flatbreads or wraps |

1 Preheat the oven to 220°C/200°C fan/gas mark 7.

2 Cut the potatoes into small fries, leaving the skin on, and tip into a large bowl. Mix with 1 tablespoon of olive oil, a pinch of salt and pepper, and 1 teaspoon of the oregano, then lay out on a baking tray and cook for 20–25 minutes, turning occasionally, until golden brown.

3 Chop the mushrooms into 1cm slices and add to a bowl. Grate in 2 garlic cloves, then add the paprika, cumin and the remaining 1 teaspoon of oregano. Mix and leave to marinate for 8–10 minutes.

4 To make the raita, grate half the cucumber into a separate bowl and squeeze out any excess liquid. Drain the excess liquid, then add the coconut yoghurt to the bowl. Finely grate in the remaining garlic clove, then squeeze in half the lemon juice. Season with a pinch of salt and pepper and set aside.

5 To prepare the salad, finely slice the red onion, chop the tomato and the remaining cucumber into small chunks, and add to a large bowl. Drizzle with olive oil and a pinch of salt and pepper and mix.

6 Heat a drizzle of vegetable oil in a frying pan over a high heat. Add the mushrooms and fry for 5–6 minutes until golden. Remove from the pan and set aside.

7 Using the same pan, lightly toast the flatbreads for 30 seconds on each side. To build the flatbreads, spread a tablespoon of the cucumber raita on to the base, then add the fries, the mushrooms and some salad. Finish with another spoonful of sauce. Serve alongside the remaining Greek salad and fries.

# Wild mushroom and leek risotto

| | |
|---|---|
| 1 | Onion |
| 1 | Leek |
| 2 | Vegetable stock cubes |
| 1 tbsp | Nutritional yeast |
| 1 tsp | Miso paste |
| 3 | Garlic cloves |
| 150g | Arborio rice |
| 250g | Wild mushrooms |
| 40g | Plant-based butter |
| Handful | Parsley |
| 1 | Lemon |

1   Finely chop the onion and trim and finely slice the leek. Heat a drizzle of olive oil in a deep-sided frying pan over a medium heat. Add the onion and leek, along with a pinch of salt, and cook for 4–5 minutes until they begin to soften.

2   Meanwhile, in a measuring jug, dissolve the stock cubes, nutritional yeast and miso paste in 800ml boiling water. Crush two of the garlic cloves. Once the leek and onion have softened, add the crushed garlic and arborio rice to the pan and cook for 1–2 minutes, then gradually add the stock, adding about 100ml at a time and letting each addition absorb into the rice before you add more, until the rice is cooked through and all the liquid is absorbed. This should take 20–25 minutes.

3   Tear or slice the wild mushrooms into smaller pieces. Once the risotto is almost ready, heat a drizzle of olive oil in a separate frying pan over a medium–high heat. Once hot, add the mushrooms and cook for 2 minutes, then add half of the plant-based butter. Crush the remaining garlic clove and add to the pan. Season with salt and pepper and cook for a further 1–2 minutes until golden. Set aside.

4   To finish the risotto, finely chop the parsley and stir half of it through the rice. Cut the lemon in half and squeeze one half into the risotto, then stir in the remaining plant-based butter. Season to taste with salt and pepper. Stir the remaining parsley through the mushrooms.

5   Serve the risotto in bowls topped with the wild mushrooms. Drizzle with a little olive oil and finish with a pinch of pepper and the remaining lemon, cut into wedges.

# Sri Lankan-style butternut and aubergine curry

| | |
|---|---|
| 1 | Butternut squash |
| 1 | Aubergine |
| 150g | Basmati rice |
| 30g | Flaked almonds |
| 1 | Red onion |
| 2 tbsp | Tomato purée |
| 2 tbsp | Sri Lankan spice blend (any medium curry blend is also fine) |
| 400g tin | Chickpeas |
| 1 | Vegetable stock cube |
| Handful | Coriander |
| 400ml | Coconut milk |

1   Peel, deseed and chop the butternut squash into 2cm cubes. Cut the aubergine into slightly larger 3cm chunks. Combine them on a large roasting tray with 1 tablespoon of vegetable oil and a pinch of salt and pepper. Roast for 20–25 minutes until soft and golden.

2   Meanwhile, in a sieve, rinse the rice with cold water, then tip into a saucepan and cover with 250ml boiling water. Cover and bring to the boil over a high heat, then reduce the heat to low and leave to cook for 10–12 minutes. Once all the water has evaporated, take off the heat and set aside.

3   Toast the flaked almonds in a dry, deep-sided frying pan over a medium heat for 2 minutes until golden, then set aside in a bowl. Dice the red onion. Return the frying pan to a medium heat and add a drizzle of vegetable oil. Add the onion and cook for 5–6 minutes until soft. Stir in the tomato purée, followed by the Sri Lankan spice blend, and cook for a further minute. Add the chickpeas (no need to drain), then crumble in the stock cube. Reduce the heat to low and simmer for 10–12 minutes.

4   Roughly chop the coriander. Add the coconut milk to the curry sauce, followed by the roasted butternut squash and aubergine. Simmer for a final 2–3 minutes (add a touch more water if you need it). Serve the curry alongside the rice, topped with the chopped coriander and the flaked almonds.

# Shepherdless pie with rich mushrooms, lentils and creamy mash

| | |
|---|---|
| 3 | Large potatoes |
| 1 | Onion |
| 1 | Carrot |
| 250g | Chestnut mushrooms |
| 2 | Garlic cloves |
| 1 tsp | Mixed Italian herbs |
| 1 tbsp | Tomato purée |
| 400g | Tin lentils |
| 1 | Vegetable stock cube |
| 1 tbsp | Soy sauce |
| 1 tbsp | Henderson's Relish |
| 1 tbsp | Onion jam or relish |
| 30g | Plant-based butter |
| 1 tbsp | Nutritional yeast |
| 200g | Tenderstem broccoli |

1 Peel the potatoes and add them to a large saucepan with plenty of boiling water and a good pinch of salt. Boil for 15 minutes or until soft and mashable, then drain and return to the pot to steam dry.

2 Finely dice the onion, and peel and finely chop the carrot. Heat with a drizzle of olive oil in a large, deep-sided frying pan over a medium heat. Add the onion and carrot, along with a pinch of salt, and cook for 4–5 minutes until starting to soften. Meanwhile, slice the mushrooms.

3 Add the mushrooms to the pan and cook for a further 4–5 minutes. Crush the garlic and add to the pan, along with the Italian herbs, tomato purée and lentils (no need to drain). Cook for 1 minute more, then crumble in the stock cube. Add 250ml of boiled water, followed by the soy sauce, Henderson's Relish and onion jam. Increase the heat to medium–high and cook for 7–8 minutes until thickened but still saucy. Season generously with salt and pepper.

4 Preheat the grill to high. To make the mash, add the plant-based butter to the drained potatoes, season generously with salt and mash until smooth. Transfer the lentil mixture to an ovenproof dish and top evenly with the mash. Brush with a little olive oil, sprinkle over the nutritional yeast and grill for 8–10 minutes until golden and crisp.

5 Meanwhile, boil the Tenderstem broccoli in a pan of boiling water over a high heat for 3–4 minutes, then drain and season with a pinch of salt and pepper. Serve the shepherdless pie with the broccoli on the side.

# Classic mushroom lasagne with dressed rocket

| | |
|---|---|
| 1 | Onion |
| 1 | Carrot |
| 250g | Chestnut mushrooms |
| 2 | Garlic cloves |
| 1 tsp | Dried oregano |
| 1 tbsp | Tomato purée |
| 1 tbsp | Balsamic vinegar |
| 1 tbsp | Soy sauce |
| 1 | Vegetable stock cube |
| ½ tbsp | Plain flour |
| 250ml | Plant-based cream |
| 6 | Lasagne sheets |
| 1 tbsp | Nutritional yeast |
| Handful | Rocket |

1 Peel and dice the onion and carrot. Heat a drizzle of olive oil in a deep-sided frying pan over a medium heat. Add the onion and carrot, along with a pinch of salt, and cook for 4 minutes until starting to soften.

2 Meanwhile, slice half the mushrooms and coarsely grate the rest. Crush the garlic. Increase the heat to high and add the mushrooms, garlic and oregano to the pan. Cook for 4 minutes more until softened.

3 Reduce the heat and add the tomato purée, balsamic vinegar and soy sauce. Crumble in the stock cube, and add 300ml boiled water. Stir and simmer for 4 minutes until slightly thickened but still saucy.

4 To make the béchamel, heat a drizzle of olive oil in a saucepan over a medium heat and add the flour. Stir for 30 seconds until nicely combined, then add the plant-based cream, along with a generous pinch of salt and pepper, and allow to thicken for 2–3 minutes.

5 Spread a small amount of the mushroom ragù into a 20 x 15cm ovenproof dish, then add a layer of 2 lasagne sheets and spoon over more ragù. Repeat the process until everything is used up, making sure to finish with lasagne sheets as the top layer. Pour over the béchamel sauce and spread until everything's fully covered. Sprinkle over the nutritional yeast and bake for 25 minutes.

6 Serve the lasagne with the rocket on the side, drizzled with olive oil and balsamic vinegar and seasoned with a pinch of salt and pepper.

# Four-bean chilli-loaded sweet potatoes topped with zingy guacamole and harissa mayo

| | |
|---|---|
| 2 | Sweet potatoes |
| 1 | Onion |
| 400g | Mixed beans |
| 1 | Vegetable stock cube |
| 1 tbsp | Mexican spice blend |
| 1 tbsp | Tomato purée |
| 1 tbsp | Rose harissa (plus 1 tsp to serve) |
| 1 | Avocado |
| 1 | Lime |
| 1 | Large tomato |
| 1 tbsp | Plant-based mayo |

1 Preheat the oven to 220°C/200°C fan/gas mark 7.

2 Prick the sweet potatoes all over with a fork and microwave them on high for 8–10 minutes until softened. Add the softened sweet potatoes to a baking tray and drizzle them with vegetable oil. Season generously with salt and bake for 15–20 minutes until crispy (if you don't have a microwave, bake for 35–40 minutes).

3 Meanwhile, dice the onion. Heat a drizzle of olive oil in a frying pan over a medium heat and add half the onion (set the rest aside in a small bowl for later). Add a pinch of salt and cook for 3–4 minutes until softened.

4 Drain and rinse the mixed beans, and dissolve the stock cube in a jug of 300ml boiling water. Add the Mexican spice blend to the softened onion and cook for 1 minute, then add the tomato purée, harissa, stock and beans, and bring to the boil. Simmer for 4–5 minutes until thickened to a chilli-like consistency.

5 To make the guac, peel, stone and finely chop the avocado and add it to the bowl with the reserved onion. Squeeze in the juice of half the lime, season with salt and mix together. Dice the tomato and stir it through.

6 To serve, carefully cut the sweet potatoes in half and open them up. Top with the four-bean chilli and dollops of guac. Finish with spoonfuls of mayo and harissa, then garnish with the remaining lime, cut into wedges.

# Fakeaway treats

# That Friday night feeling, minus the questionable meats.

30 mins
Serves 2

# Crispy chilli and sesame tofu with aromatic green beans

| | |
|---|---|
| 280g | Firm tofu |
| 1 tbsp | Soy sauce |
| 2 tbsp | Cornflour |
| 150g | Basmati rice |
| 1 tbsp | Sriracha |
| 1 tbsp | Rose harissa |
| 1 tbsp | Agave syrup |
| 3 cloves | Garlic |
| 30g | Fresh ginger |
| 200g | Green beans |
| 1 tsp | Sesame seeds |

1 Break the tofu into small bite-sized pieces and place into a large bowl. Pour in the soy sauce and give it a good mix. Leave to soak for 2–3 minutes, before adding in the cornflour and mixing well to ensure all the pieces are coated. Preheat a large frying pan with vegetable oil, before adding the tofu pieces. Gently move them around the pan, turning every few minutes so that they crisp on all sides.

2 Rinse the rice with cold water, place into a saucepan and cover with 300ml boiling water. Bring the rice to the boil over a high heat with the lid on, then turn down to a low simmer and leave to cook for 10–12 minutes. Once all the water has evaporated, take off the heat and set aside.

3 In a small bowl, mix together the sriracha, harissa paste, agave syrup, 1 clove of garlic (peeled and crushed) and a drizzle of oil. Mix well then set to one side. Finely chop the remaining garlic and ginger. Mix the chilli sauce through the crispy tofu.

4 Top and tail the green beans and place into a frying pan with 100ml boiling water. Steam-fry them until the water has evaporated. Add the chopped garlic and ginger and a drizzle of oil and gently fry for 4–5 minutes until aromatic. Sprinkle over the sesame seeds and continue to gently fry the veg. Season with a pinch of salt.

5 Serve the crispy tofu alongside the steamed rice and the aromatic green beans.

# 'Nduja and broccoli pizza-style crispy flatbreads

| | |
|---|---|
| 200g | Tenderstem broccoli |
| 2 | Garlic cloves |
| 4 | Flatbreads |
| 1 tbsp | Tomato purée |
| 1 tsp | Dried oregano |
| 100g | Plant-based cheese |
| 2 tbsp | Plant-based 'nduja |
| 1 tsp | Fennel seeds |
| 1 tbsp | Balsamic vinegar |
| 1 | Shallot |
| 250g | Cherry tomatoes |
| Handful | Rocket |

1 Preheat the oven to 220°C/200°C fan/gas mark 7.

2 Chop the Tenderstem broccoli into thirds, setting aside some of the thinner heads and stalks to top your pizzas. Add the remaining broccoli to a saucepan of boiling water and cook for 2–3 minutes until tender, then drain and set aside to cool.

3 Crush the garlic into a small bowl and add 3 tablespoons olive oil and a pinch of salt and pepper. Stir to combine. Place two of the flatbreads on a large baking tray and spread them evenly with the garlic oil. Top each with the remaining flatbreads and press down to stick together.

4 Add the tomato purée to the empty garlic oil bowl and mix with the oregano, 3 tablespoons water and a pinch of salt and pepper. Spread this tomato sauce over the top flatbreads. Top with the grated cheese, dollops of the plant-based 'nduja and the reserved broccoli, then sprinkle over the fennel seeds. Drizzle with a little olive oil and bake for 10–12 minutes until golden and crisp.

5 For the salad, add the balsamic vinegar to a large bowl with 3 tablespoons olive oil and a pinch of salt and pepper. Finely slice the shallot and halve the cherry tomatoes. Add the rocket, cherry tomatoes, shallot and cooled broccoli to the bowl and mix together.

6 Serve the flatbread pizzas with the salad alongside.

25 mins
Serves 2

# Aubergine and green bean Thai curry topped with fresh lime, chilli and coriander

| | |
|---|---|
| 150g | Basmati rice |
| 1 | Aubergine |
| 200g | Green beans |
| 1 | Red pepper |
| 1 | Banana shallot |
| 1 tbsp | Thai green curry paste |
| 400ml | Coconut milk |
| ½ tsp | Ground turmeric |
| 1 | Vegetable stock cube |
| Handful | Coriander |
| 1 | Red chilli |
| 1 | Lime |

1  In a sieve, rinse the rice with cold water, then tip into a saucepan and cover with 300ml boiling water. Cover and bring to the boil over a high heat, then reduce the heat to low and leave to simmer for 10–12 minutes. Once all the water has evaporated, take off the heat and set aside.

2  Meanwhile, cut the aubergine into wedges (lengthways). Trim and halve the green beans. Deseed and finely slice the red pepper.

3  Heat a drizzle of vegetable oil in a deep-sided frying pan over a high heat. Add the aubergine and a pinch of salt, and fry for 2–3 minutes until the outsides are golden. Pour in 100ml boiling water and cover the pan with a lid. Steam-fry the aubergine for 3–4 minutes until all the water has evaporated, then remove from the pan and set aside.

4  Finely slice the shallot and add to the now-empty pan. Fry for 2 minutes before adding the Thai green curry paste and 1 teaspoon vegetable oil. Fry for a minute more to release the flavour of the paste, then stir in the aubergine, red pepper and green beans. Add the coconut milk and turmeric, and crumble in the stock cube. Stir and bring to the boil, then reduce the heat to low and simmer for 10 minutes until all the veg is tender.

5  Finely chop the coriander and red chilli. Serve the cooked rice in bowls, topped with the Thai green curry. Finish with a good squeeze of the lime and scatter over the chopped coriander and red chilli.

# Black bean enchiladas with 'cheesy' topping and guacamole

| | |
|---|---|
| 1 | Red onion |
| 250g | Cherry tomatoes |
| 1 | Green chilli |
| 1 | Lime |
| 400g tin | Black beans |
| 1 tbsp | Smoked paprika |
| 1 tsp | Ground cumin |
| 1 tbsp | Tomato purée |
| 1 | Vegetable stock cube |
| 6 | Tortilla wraps |
| 50g | Plant-based cheese |
| 1 | Avocado |
| Handful | Coriander |

1 Preheat the oven to 220°C/200°C fan/gas mark 7.

2 Finely dice the red onion, quarter the cherry tomatoes and finely chop the green chilli. Add half the onion to a small bowl with half the tomatoes and half the chopped chilli. Squeeze in the lime juice, and add a drizzle of olive oil and a pinch of salt. Stir to combine into a salsa and set aside.

3 Heat a drizzle of olive oil in a frying pan over a medium heat. Add the remaining onion with a pinch of salt and cook for 4–5 minutes. Drain and rinse the black beans and add to the pan, along with the remaining tomatoes and chilli. Stir in the smoked paprika and ground cumin and cook for 1 minute, then add the tomato purée and 250ml boiling water. Crumble in the stock cube and cook for 4–5 minutes until thickened.

4 Lightly grease an ovenproof dish with olive oil. Heat the tortillas in the microwave for 30 seconds until warm (or in a dry pan over a medium heat for a minute). Divide the black bean mixture between the tortillas, then roll them up and nestle them into the dish. Grate the plant-based cheese over the top. Bake for 10–12 minutes or until crisp.

5 Meanwhile, peel, stone and smash the avocado with a fork. Finely chop the coriander. Mix the tomato salsa with the smashed avocado and chopped coriander to make your guac.

6 Dollop some of the guac over the enchiladas, then serve the rest in a small bowl on the side for dipping.

# Sticky tofu, cashew and pepper stir-fry with sesame seeds and basmati rice

| | |
|---|---|
| 150g | Basmati rice |
| 280g | Firm tofu |
| 1 | Red pepper |
| 2 | Spring onions |
| 2 | Garlic cloves |
| 30g | Fresh ginger |
| 1 tbsp | Soy sauce |
| 1 tbsp | Caster sugar |
| 1 tbsp | Mirin |
| 1 tsp | Sesame seeds |
| 30g | Cashews |

1   In a sieve, rinse the rice with cold water, then tip into a saucepan and cover with 300ml boiling water. Cover and bring to the boil over a high heat, then reduce the heat to low and leave to simmer for 10–12 minutes. Once all the water has evaporated, take off the heat and set aside.

2   Meanwhile, heat a drizzle of vegetable oil in a large, deep-sided frying pan over a high heat. Pat dry the tofu, then chop into 1cm cubes. Chop the red pepper into small pieces, and finely slice the spring onions. Once the pan is hot, add the tofu, red pepper, and half the spring onions. Fry for 4–5 minutes until starting to colour.

3   Meanwhile, in a small bowl, crush the garlic and peel and grate the ginger. Add the soy sauce, sugar, mirin and sesame seeds, and mix well.

4   Once the tofu and veg have coloured, pour over the sauce and add the cashews. Mix well, adding a splash of water to loosen if needed. Continue to fry for a further 4–5 minutes.

5   Once the rice is cooked, serve alongside the cashew and pepper stir-fry, garnished with the remaining spring onions.

# Spanish tortilla with roasted pepper salad and garlic-and-herb aioli

| | |
|---|---|
| 1 | Red pepper |
| 3 | Potatoes |
| 1 | Onion |
| 100g | Gram flour |
| 1 tbsp | Nutritional yeast |
| 1 tbsp | White wine vinegar |
| 1 | Tomato |
| Handful | Rocket |
| 30g | Pitted green olives |
| Handful | Parsley |
| 2 | Garlic cloves |
| 1 tbsp | Plant-based mayo |

1 Preheat the oven to 220°C/200°C fan/gas mark 7. Line an ovenproof dish (round if possible) with baking paper.

2 Chop the red pepper into large wedges and add to a baking tray with a drizzle of olive oil and a pinch of salt. Roast for 20 minutes until softened and starting to char.

3 Meanwhile, peel and chop the potatoes into 1cm cubes, and finely slice the onion. Heat a very generous drizzle of olive oil in a large, deep-sided frying pan over a medium–high heat. Once hot, add the potatoes and fry for 10 minutes, stirring every so often until starting to soften and lightly colour.

4 Meanwhile, add the gram flour to a large bowl with 200ml cold water, the nutritional yeast and a generous pinch of salt. Whisk to make a smooth batter.

5 Once the potatoes have had 10 minutes, add the sliced onion and fry for 8 minutes more, then carefully transfer the softened potatoes and onion to the prepared baking dish. Pour the batter over the top, making sure everything is evenly covered, and bake for 15 minutes or until set.

6 To make the salad, add the vinegar to a large bowl with 2 tablespoons of olive oil and a good pinch of salt and pepper. Chop the tomato into wedges and add to the bowl, along with the rocket and olives. To make the herby aioli, finely chop the parsley and crush the garlic, and add both to a small bowl with the mayo. Loosen with a small splash of water.

7 Serve slabs of the Spanish tortilla alongside the roasted red pepper, dressed salad and aioli.

# Satay-glazed aubergine with spicy green bean, peanut and carrot salad

| | |
|---|---|
| 1 | Aubergine |
| 150g | Basmati rice |
| 200g | Green beans |
| 1 | Red chilli |
| 1 | Large carrot |
| 3 | Spring onions |
| Handful | Coriander |
| 30g | Unsalted peanuts |
| 1 tbsp | Sesame oil |
| 1 | Lime |
| 1 tbsp | Agave syrup |
| 1 tbsp | Miso paste |
| 2 tbsp | Smooth peanut butter |

1 Preheat the oven to 220°C/200°C fan/gas mark 7.

2 Slice the aubergine in half lengthways, then slice lengthways almost up to the stem so that each half stays attached at the stem, and fan out on a roasting tray. Drizzle with vegetable oil and season with a pinch of salt and pepper. Roast for 20 minutes.

3 Meanwhile, in a sieve, rinse the rice with cold water, then tip into a saucepan and cover with 300ml boiling water. Cover and bring to the boil over a high heat, then reduce the heat to low and leave to simmer for 10–12 minutes. Once all the water has evaporated, take off the heat and set aside.

4 Bring another saucepan of water to the boil. Trim and halve the green beans. Boil for 2–3 minutes, then drain and rinse with cold water. Add to a large bowl. Finely dice the red chilli and add half to the bowl (keep the rest back for the satay sauce). Peel and grate the carrot, slice the spring onions and chop the coriander, then add these to the bowl as well, along with the peanuts and sesame oil. Mix and set aside.

5 For the satay sauce, squeeze the lime into a small bowl, then stir in the agave syrup, miso paste, peanut butter and remaining chopped chilli. Take 1 tablespoon to stir through the green bean salad, then pour the remaining satay sauce over the roasted aubergine. Return the aubergine to the oven for 2 minutes to warm through.

6 Serve the satay-glazed aubergine alongside the rice and green bean salad.

# Oyster mushroom 'calamari' with pan con tomate, rocket and garlic aioli

| | |
|---|---|
| 400g | Oyster mushrooms |
| 1 tbsp | Soy sauce |
| 1 | Lemon |
| 1 | Large tomato |
| 2 | Garlic cloves |
| 2 tbsp | Plant-based mayo |
| 2 | Ciabatta rolls |
| 3 tbsp | Cornflour |
| Handful | Rocket |

1   To make the 'calamari', tip the mushrooms into a large bowl, tearing any larger ones in half. Add the soy sauce and a generous pinch of pepper. Halve the lemon and squeeze in the juice of one half (cut the other half into wedges for later). Mix and set aside to marinate.

2   Chop the tomato in half and coarsely grate the flesh into a large bowl, discarding the skin as you go. Season the grated tomato with a generous pinch of salt and pepper, and add 1½ tablespoons of olive oil. To make the aioli, crush the garlic into a small bowl and mix with the mayo and a small splash of water. Set both aside.

3   Cut the ciabatta rolls into thin slices. Heat a drizzle of olive oil in a large frying pan over a medium–high heat. Add the ciabatta slices and cook for 1–2 minutes on each side until golden and crisp, then set aside.

4   Add the cornflour to the marinated mushrooms and mix until fully coated. Return the now-empty pan to a medium–high heat and add a generous drizzle of vegetable oil (enough to cover the base of the pan). Once hot, add the coated mushrooms and cook for 7–8 minutes, turning until fully golden and crisp. For the perfect crisp, do this in batches.

5   To serve, spread the ciabatta slices with the seasoned tomato pulp and serve alongside the oyster mushroom 'calamari' and aioli. Drizzle the rocket with some olive oil and add to the plates, with the lemon wedges on the side for squeezing.

# Creamy cashew and sweet potato korma with basmati rice

| | |
|---|---|
| 1 | Sweet potato |
| 400g tin | Chickpeas |
| 150g | Basmati rice |
| ½ | Lime |
| 30g | Fresh ginger |
| 1 tbsp | Rose harissa |
| 1 tbsp | Tomato purée |
| 2 tsp | Mild curry powder |
| 30g | Cashews |
| 1 tbsp | Mango chutney |
| 1 | Onion |
| 2 | Garlic cloves |
| 400ml | Coconut milk |
| Handful | Baby spinach |

1   Preheat the oven to 200°C/180°C fan/gas mark 6.

2   Cut the sweet potato into bite-sized pieces and tip on to a baking tray. Drain the chickpeas and add them to the tray, along with a drizzle of vegetable oil and a pinch of salt. Mix well and roast for 20–25 minutes until the sweet potato is tender.

3   In a sieve, rinse the rice with cold water, then tip into a saucepan and cover with 300ml boiling water. Cover and bring to the boil over a high heat, then reduce the heat to low and leave to simmer for 10–12 minutes. Once all the water has evaporated, take off the heat and set aside.

4   Meanwhile, squeeze the lime juice into a blender, and then add the ginger, harissa, tomato purée, curry powder, cashews and mango chutney. Blend until it forms a smooth paste (add a little water if necessary).

5   Finely dice the onion and garlic. Heat a drizzle of vegetable oil in a large, deep-sided frying pan over a medium heat. Add the onion and garlic and season with a pinch of salt. Fry for 2–3 minutes until softening, then stir in the blended curry paste and cook for a further minute to allow the spices to cook out. Add the coconut milk and leave to simmer for 10–12 minutes.

6   Once the roasted veg is ready, add it to the curry sauce, along with the spinach, and mix well. Add a little water if the curry is too stiff. Leave to gently simmer until the spinach is wilted. Serve the curry alongside the rice.

# Crispy tofu bánh mì with pickled slaw, sriracha mayo and fries

| | |
|---|---|
| 2 | Large potatoes |
| 280g | Firm tofu |
| 1 tbsp | Soy sauce |
| 2 tbsp | Cornflour |
| Handful | Coriander |
| 1 | Green chilli |
| 1 | Lime |
| 1 tbsp | Rice vinegar |
| 1 tbsp | Sriracha |
| 3 tbsp | Plant-based mayo |
| 2 | Ciabatta rolls |
| 1 | Carrot |
| Handful | Radishes |

1 Preheat the oven to 220°C/200°C fan/gas mark 7.

2 Cut the potatoes into fries and arrange them on a baking tray. Drizzle with vegetable oil and season with a pinch of salt, then bake for 25–30 minutes until golden and crisp.

3 Meanwhile, cut the tofu in half, then slice each half into 6 slices. Add the tofu slices to a large bowl with the soy sauce and gently mix together. Sprinkle over the cornflour and toss to coat, then set aside.

4 Pick the coriander leaves from their stalks and set aside for serving. Finely chop the stalks and finely slice the green chilli. Zest the lime into a separate large bowl and add the rice vinegar, along with half the green chilli slices and the coriander stalks. Set aside. In a small bowl, mix together the sriracha and mayo with a squeeze of lime.

5 Heat a generous drizzle of vegetable oil in a large frying pan over a medium–high heat. Once hot, add the coated tofu and fry for 10 minutes, turning every few minutes until really golden and crispy.

6 Meanwhile, cut the ciabatta rolls in half and put them in the oven for 4–5 minutes to warm through. Grate the carrot and radishes into the large bowl of lime zest and rice vinegar, season with salt and mix to combine.

7 Spread the ciabatta bases with the sriracha mayo, then top with the crispy tofu and some of the pickled veg. Top with a bundle of coriander leaves, the remaining green chilli slices and a squeeze of lime. Serve with the fries and remaining pickled veg on the side.

# Mexican bean tostadas with zingy sweetcorn salsa

| | |
|---|---|
| 400g | Oyster mushrooms |
| 1 tbsp | Soy sauce |
| 1 tsp | Smoked paprika |
| 2 | Garlic cloves |
| 1 | Red onion |
| 400g tin | Pinto beans |
| 1½ tsp | Mexican spice blend |
| 1 | Red chilli |
| 1 | Lime |
| 200g tin | Sweetcorn |
| Handful | Coriander |
| 6 | Mini tortilla wraps |

1   Tear the oyster mushrooms into strips and place in a large bowl with the soy sauce and smoked paprika. Finely chop one of the garlic cloves and add to the bowl. Mix well and set aside to marinate.

2   Finely dice the red onion. Heat a drizzle of vegetable oil in a frying pan over a medium heat. Add half the diced onion, along with a pinch of salt. Fry for 2–3 minutes until softened, then drain and rinse the pinto beans and add to the pan, along with the Mexican spice blend. Fry for 2–3 minutes more, then pour in 100ml boiling water. Season with a pinch of salt and leave to simmer for 4–5 minutes. Once they are soft, use the back of a fork to mash the pinto beans into a rough paste. Take off the heat and set aside.

3   For the salsa, finely dice the red chilli and add to a bowl with the remaining diced onion. Squeeze in the juice of the lime, then drain the sweetcorn and tip this in too. Roughly chop half the coriander and add to the bowl. Mix well, and season to taste with salt and pepper.

4   Heat a drizzle of vegetable oil in a separate frying pan over a medium–high heat. Add the marinated mushrooms and fry for 4–5 minutes until they are softened and golden brown in colour. Once ready, remove from the pan and set aside. Using the same pan on the same heat, fry the tortilla wraps on one side until golden brown in colour and starting to crisp.

5   To assemble the tostadas, spread each wrap with the pinto bean paste, then top with spoonfuls of the sweetcorn salsa, and finish with the mushrooms and fresh coriander leaves.

# Patatas bravas and tofu nuggets with garlic aioli, homemade tomato sauce and pan-fried little gems

| | |
|---|---|
| 280g | Firm tofu |
| 1 tbsp | Soy sauce |
| 1 | Onion |
| 500g | New potatoes |
| 2 | Garlic cloves |
| 2 tsp | Smoked paprika |
| 1 tbsp | Sun-dried tomato purée |
| 1 | Vegetable stock cube |
| 2 tbsp | Cornflour |
| 1 tsp | Dried oregano |
| 1 tbsp | Plant-based mayo |
| 2 | Little gem lettuce |
| 1 | Lemon |

1   Preheat the oven to 220°C/200°C fan/gas mark 7.

2   Tear the tofu into bite-sized pieces and place them in a bowl. Pour over the soy sauce and mix well, then leave to marinate for 2–3 minutes. Meanwhile, chop half the onion into thin wedges and place in a baking tray. Cut the potatoes into bite-sized pieces and add them to the tray. Season with a pinch of salt and pepper and generously drizzle with olive oil. Roast for 20–25 minutes until golden.

3   Finely dice the remaining onion and crush 1 garlic clove. Fry the onion on a medium-high heat 3–4 minutes until starting to soften. Add the crushed garlic, 1 teaspoon of the smoked paprika and the sun-dried tomato purée. Crumble in the stock cube and pour over 150ml boiling water. Stir well and bring to the boil, then reduce the heat to low and simmer for 6–7 minutes until thickened. Season to taste.

4   Add the cornflour, oregano and the remaining smoked paprika to the tofu and mix well. Heat a generous glug of vegetable oil in a large frying pan over a medium heat. Once hot, carefully place the tofu pieces into the pan and fry for 6–7 minutes, turning occasionally until golden all over.

5   Grate the remaining garlic clove into a small bowl. Add the mayo and a dash of water to thin it slightly, then mix well and season to taste with salt and pepper.

6   Transfer the cooked tofu to a plate, then fry the little gem wedges in the pan for 2–3 minutes until golden.

7   Serve the potatoes topped with the tomato and garlic sauce, alongside the tofu nuggets and charred little gem wedges. Finish with a good squeeze of lemon.

30 mins
Serves 2

# Sticky mango tofu skewers with sticky coconut rice and charred sweetcorn salsa

| | |
|---|---|
| 1 | Vegetable stock cube |
| 50g | Creamed coconut |
| 150g | Basmati rice |
| 200g tin | Sweetcorn |
| 280g | Firm tofu |
| 1 tbsp | Soy sauce |
| 2 tbsp | Cornflour |
| 1 | Large tomato |
| 1 | Red onion |
| Handful | Coriander |
| 1 | Lime |
| 2 tbsp | Mango chutney |

1  In a measuring jug, dissolve the stock cube and creamed coconut in 350ml boiled water. Add the rice to a saucepan with the coconut stock and bring to the boil over a high heat. Once boiling, reduce the heat to low and cook, covered, for 15–17 minutes until the rice is cooked and all the liquid has been absorbed.

2  Meanwhile, heat a drizzle of vegetable oil in a large frying pan over a high heat. Drain the sweetcorn and add it to the pan. Cook for 5–6 minutes until charred, then transfer to a large bowl and set aside.

3  Pat dry the tofu, then tear it into large chunks. Tip it into a separate large bowl and add the soy sauce. Mix well, then sprinkle over the cornflour and toss to fully coat.

4  Return the now-empty pan to a medium–high heat with a generous drizzle of vegetable oil. Once hot, add the tofu (you can thread it on to skewers first, if you wish) and cook for 7–8 minutes, turning occasionally, until golden brown and crisp.

5  Meanwhile, finely dice the tomato and red onion. Finely chop the coriander (saving some leaves for garnish). Add the tomato, onion and chopped coriander to the bowl with the charred corn. Add a drizzle of olive oil, squeeze in the juice of the lime and season with a good pinch of salt and pepper. In a separate small bowl, mix the mango chutney with 1 tablespoon water to loosen.

6  Serve the crispy tofu alongside the coconut rice and charred sweetcorn salsa. Drizzle the mango chutney over the tofu and garnish with the remaining coriander leaves.

# Oyster mushroom birria tacos with ancho dipping sauce

| | |
|---|---|
| 400g | Oyster mushrooms |
| 1 | Onion |
| 2 | Garlic cloves |
| 1 tsp | Ancho chilli powder (or smoked paprika) |
| 1 tbsp | Tomato purée |
| 1 tsp | Chipotle paste |
| 1 | Vegetable stock cube |
| 6 | Tortilla wraps |
| 100g | Plant-based cheese |
| Handful | Coriander |
| 1 | Lime |

1   Preheat the oven to 220°C/200°C fan/gas mark 7.

2   Tear the oyster mushrooms into thin strips. Dice the onion and finely slice the garlic. Heat a drizzle of olive oil in a deep-sided frying pan over a high heat. Add the shredded mushrooms and a pinch of salt, and cook for 3–4 minutes, stirring occasionally, until starting to brown. Add half the sliced garlic and cook for 1 minute more. Transfer to a plate and set aside.

3   Return the now-empty pan to a medium heat and add half the diced onion, along with the remaining garlic and a pinch of salt. Add the ancho chilli powder and cook for 3 minutes, then add the tomato purée and chipotle paste. Crumble in the stock cube and pour in 300ml boiling water. Simmer for 4–5 minutes until starting to thicken.

4   Line a large tray with baking paper. Remove the thickened sauce from the heat and dip the tortilla wraps into it one by one until fully coated and place onto the tray.

5   Divide the cooked mushrooms between the tortilla wraps, covering only half, then grate over the plant-based cheese. Fold the tortillas into half-moon shapes, press them down to close and arrange them on the prepared baking tray. Bake for 10–12 minutes until golden and crisp.

6   Finely chop the coriander and cut the lime into wedges. Stir most of the coriander through the remaining sauce. Serve the birria tacos with the sauce in little bowls on the side for dipping. Garnish with the remaining diced onion and chopped coriander, with lime wedges on the side.

# Chilli greens udon noodles with Tenderstem broccoli and pak choi

| | |
|---|---|
| 200g | Tenderstem broccoli |
| 2 | Pak choi |
| 400g | Udon noodles |
| 30g | Fresh ginger |
| 2 | Garlic cloves |
| 1 tbsp | Soy sauce |
| ½ tsp | Chilli flakes |
| 1 tbsp | Sriracha |
| 1 tbsp | Rice vinegar |
| 2 tbsp | Sesame oil |
| 1 tsp | Caster sugar |
| 2 | Spring onions |
| 1 tsp | Sesame seeds |

1 Chop the Tenderstem broccoli into thirds. Trim the roots from the pak choi and discard. Finely slice the white parts of the pak choi and separate the leaves. Heat a drizzle of vegetable oil in a large frying pan or wok over a high heat. Add the broccoli and fry for 4–5 minutes until beginning to soften.

2 Meanwhile, add the udon noodles to a large bowl and pour over enough boiled water to cover. Leave to soak for 3–4 minutes until starting to soften. Gently separate the noodles with a fork, then drain and set aside.

3 Peel and finely chop the ginger and garlic, then add to the broccoli pan, along with the pak choi whites, and cook for 1 minute. Add the pak choi leaves, followed by the soy sauce, chilli flakes, sriracha, rice vinegar, sesame oil and sugar, and cook for 1 minute to wilt the leaves.

4 Add the drained noodles to the pan and cook for a final minute, stirring to coat in the sauce.

5 Finely slice the spring onions. Serve the noodles in bowls, topped with the spring onions and sesame seeds.

# Crispy tofu burger, carrot slaw and chips with homemade chicken shop gravy

30 mins
Serves 2

| | |
|---|---|
| 2 | Potatoes |
| 280g | Firm tofu |
| 2 tbsp | Soy sauce |
| 1 tsp | Ancho chilli powder (smoked paprika also works) |
| 2 tbsp | Cornflour |
| 1 tbsp | White wine vinegar |
| 2 tbsp | Plant-based mayo |
| 1 | Carrot |
| 1 | Little gem lettuce |
| 2 | Garlic cloves |
| 1 | Vegetable stock cube |
| 1 tbsp | Nutritional yeast |
| 2 | Plant-based brioche buns |

1  Preheat the oven to 220°C/200°C fan/gas mark 7.

2  Cut the potatoes into fries and toss them on a baking tray with a drizzle of vegetable oil and a pinch of salt. Bake for 25–30 minutes until crisp.

3  Pat dry the tofu, then rip it into six strips. Add to a plate and drizzle over half the soy sauce. Sprinkle with the ancho chilli powder and toss to coat. Keep 1 teaspoon of the cornflour aside for later, and toss the rest with the tofu to coat.

4  Heat a generous drizzle of vegetable oil in a deep-sided frying pan over a medium–high heat. Add the coated tofu and cook for 10 minutes, turning until golden and crisp.

5  Meanwhile, combine the white wine vinegar and half the mayo in a bowl with a pinch of salt. Grate the carrot and shred the lettuce and set aside.

6  To make the gravy, heat a drizzle of olive oil in a saucepan over a medium heat and add the remaining cornflour. Crush in the garlic and cook for 30 seconds. Crumble in the stock cube, then add 200ml boiling water, along with the nutritional yeast and remaining soy sauce. Stir and simmer for 5 minutes until thickened. Meanwhile, add the brioche buns to the oven to warm through for 3–4 minutes.

7  To build the burgers, spread the base of each bun with the remaining mayo, then top with shredded lettuce, followed by the crispy tofu and a drizzle of gravy. Add the grated carrot and remaining lettuce to the bowl with the mayo and toss to make a slaw. Serve alongside the burgers and chips, with any remaining gravy on the side for dipping.

# Butternut squash and pinto 'quesadillas' with avocado salsa and coconut-lime sauce

| | |
|---|---|
| 1 | Butternut squash |
| 1 tbsp | Mexican spice blend |
| 1 | Red onion |
| 1 | Red pepper |
| 400g tin | Pinto beans |
| 250g | Cherry tomatoes |
| Handful | Coriander |
| 1 | Avocado |
| 1 | Lime |
| 1 tbsp | Coconut yoghurt |
| 4 | Tortilla wraps |

1   Preheat the oven to 220°C/200°C fan/gas mark 7.

2   Peel, deseed and chop the butternut squash into 2cm cubes. Toss on a baking tray with half the Mexican spice blend and a drizzle of vegetable oil, and roast for 25–30 minutes until tender.

3   Slice the red onion and red pepper into strips. Heat a drizzle of vegetable oil in a large frying pan over a medium heat. Add the onion and red pepper and cook for 5–7 minutes until softened. Stir in the rest of the Mexican spice blend. Reduce the heat to low, then drain and rinse the pinto beans and add to the pan, along with 100ml boiling water. Leave to gently simmer while you prepare everything else.

4   For the salsa, chop the tomatoes into quarters and roughly chop the coriander. Peel, stone and chop the avocado. Mix together in a bowl and squeeze in half of the lime juice. Season with a pinch of salt and pepper.

5   For the coconut sauce, tip the coconut yoghurt into a small bowl and squeeze in the remaining lime juice.

6   When the butternut squash is nearly ready, tip the bean mixture into the roasting tray for the final 5 minutes in the oven. Wipe out the frying pan, and, over a high heat, toast the tortilla wraps for 15 seconds on each side until golden.

7   To serve, spoon the butternut mix on to one half of each wrap, then top with the avocado salsa and the coconut sauce. Fold each wrap in half, press down and cut into triangles.

# Tofu tikka masala with brown rice

| | |
|---|---|
| 150g | Brown rice |
| 1 tbsp | Medium curry powder |
| 1 tsp | Garam masala |
| 1 tsp | Paprika |
| 280g | Firm tofu |
| 1 | Red onion |
| 30g | Fresh ginger |
| 1 | Large tomato |
| 1 tbsp | Tomato purée |
| 1 tsp | Caster sugar |
| 1 | Vegetable stock cube |
| 50g | Creamed coconut |
| Handful | Coriander |
| 1 tbsp | Nigella seeds (optional) |

1   In a sieve, rinse the brown rice, then tip it into a saucepan with plenty of salted boiling water. Boil for 20–25 minutes until tender with a bite, then drain and set aside with a lid on until ready to serve.

2   Meanwhile, in a small bowl, combine the curry powder, garam masala and paprika and mix well. This is your tikka spice blend. Pat dry the tofu, then tear it into large bite-sized chunks and add to a large bowl with half of the tikka spice blend. Mix well. Heat a drizzle of vegetable oil in a large, deep-sided frying pan over a medium–high heat. Add the tofu and cook for 6 minutes, turning every so often until golden all over. Once done, transfer to a bowl and set aside.

3   Meanwhile, finely dice the red onion, peel and finely chop the ginger, and roughly chop the tomato. Return the empty pan to a medium heat with a drizzle of vegetable oil, and add three-quarters of the onion and a pinch of salt. Cook for 3–4 minutes until starting to soften, then add the remaining tikka spice blend, along with the ginger and tomato. Cook for another 4–5 minutes, then add the tomato purée and sugar. Crumble in the stock cube and pour over 300ml boiling water, then simmer for 5–6 minutes until the tomatoes begin breaking down. Return the tofu to the pan, along with the creamed coconut, and stir until melted and combined.

4   Finely chop the coriander, reserving a few leaves for garnish. Stir the chopped coriander through the sauce. Serve the tofu tikka masala with the rice alongside. Garnish with the reserved coriander leaves, the remaining onion and the nigella seeds (if using).

# Smoky pulled aubergine and black bean-loaded fries with green goddess sauce

| | |
|---|---|
| 1 | Aubergine |
| 3 | Potatoes |
| 1 | Red onion |
| 2 | Garlic cloves |
| 1 tbsp | Tomato purée |
| 1 tbsp | Ancho chilli powder (or smoked paprika) |
| 1 tsp | Dried oregano |
| 400g tin | Black beans |
| 1 | Vegetable stock cube |
| 150g | Cherry tomatoes |
| 1 | Avocado |
| Handful | Coriander |
| 1 | Lime |

1 Preheat the oven to 220°C/200°C fan/gas mark 7.

2 Halve the aubergine lengthways and score the flesh in a criss-cross pattern about 1cm deep. Place on a baking tray with a drizzle of vegetable oil and roast for 20–25 minutes, until soft and melty.

3 Meanwhile, chop the potatoes into 1cm-thick fries and toss on a second baking tray with a drizzle of vegetable oil and a pinch of salt. Roast for 20–25 minutes until golden.

4 Finely dice the red onion and crush 1 garlic clove. Heat a drizzle of vegetable oil in a deep-sided pan over a medium–high heat. Add the onion and fry for 3–4 minutes until soft, then add the crushed garlic, tomato purée, ancho chilli powder and oregano. Fry for 1–2 minutes more, then drain and rinse the black beans and add to the pan. Crumble in the stock cube and pour over 200ml boiling water. Bring to the boil, then reduce the heat and leave to simmer for 15 minutes.

5 Once the aubergine is ready, remove from the oven and remove and discard the skin. Pull apart the flesh and add this to the black bean mix. Roughly chop the cherry tomatoes and add to the pan. Stir and leave to simmer while you wait for the fries to finish cooking.

6 Peel and stone the avocado and peel the remaining garlic clove. Add to a blender with two-thirds of the coriander and 3 tablespoons of water. Squeeze in the lime juice and blend until smooth. Chop the remaining coriander.

7 Serve the fries covered in the pulled aubergine mix, topped with the avocado sauce. Finish with the remaining coriander.

35 mins
Serves 2

# Sweet-and-sour tofu with umami mushroom rice

| | |
|---|---|
| 150g | Basmati rice |
| 250g | Chestnut mushrooms |
| 280g | Firm tofu |
| 2 tbsp | Cornflour |
| 1 | Red pepper |
| 1 tbsp | Agave syrup |
| 1 tbsp | Rose harissa |
| 1 tbsp | Tomato purée |
| 1 tbsp | Rice vinegar |
| 2 | Spring onions |
| 1 tbsp | Soy sauce |

1  In a sieve, rinse the rice with cold water, then tip into a saucepan and cover with 300ml boiling water. Cover and bring to the boil over a high heat, then reduce the heat to low and leave to simmer for 10–12 minutes. Once all the water has evaporated, take off the heat and set aside.

2  Finely slice the mushrooms. Heat a drizzle of vegetable oil in a large frying pan over a high heat. Add the mushrooms, along with a pinch of salt, and fry for 4–5 minutes until golden. Remove from the pan and set aside on a plate.

3  Pat dry the tofu, then rip it into bite-sized chunks and place them into a large bowl. Sprinkle the cornflour over the tofu chunks and toss them well, ensuring that they are coated evenly. Cut the red pepper into similar-sized chunks. Return the frying pan to a medium-high heat and add a drizzle of vegetable oil. Add the coated tofu and the pepper and fry for 7–8 minutes until golden brown.

4  Meanwhile, to make the sauce, mix together the agave syrup, harissa, tomato purée and rice vinegar in a small bowl. Whisk well, then pour the sauce over the cooked tofu and pepper, and stir to coat the pieces in the sauce. Leave to simmer over a low heat.

5  Finely slice the spring onions. Once the rice is cooked, stir through the fried mushrooms and soy sauce. Serve the rice on plates alongside the sticky tofu, topped with the spring onions.

# Healthy eats

# Absolutely no rabbit food to see here.

30 mins
Serves 2

# Mexican black bean stew with fresh avocado and toasted flatbreads

| | |
|---|---|
| 1 | Red onion |
| 1 | Yellow pepper |
| 1 | Vegetable stock cube |
| 1 tsp | Caster sugar |
| 400g tin | Black beans |
| 1 | Avocado |
| Handful | Coriander |
| ½ tsp | Chilli flakes |
| 1 tbsp | Mexican spice blend |
| 400g | Tomato passata |
| 4 | Tortilla wraps |
| 1 | Lime |

1 Preheat the oven to 200°C/180°C fan/gas mark 6.

2 Finely slice the red onion. Chop the yellow pepper into thin strips. Heat a drizzle of olive oil in a large pan over a medium heat. Add the yellow pepper, along with most of the sliced onion (save some for garnish) and a pinch of salt. Cook for 6–8 minutes until starting to soften.

3 Meanwhile, dissolve the stock cube and sugar in a jug with 350ml boiling water. Drain and rinse the black beans. Peel, stone and finely slice the avocado, and roughly chop the coriander.

4 Add the drained black beans to the pan with the yellow pepper strips. Stir in the chilli flakes and Mexican spice blend, and cook for 1 minute until fragrant. Add the veg stock and tomato passata, then increase the heat to high and bring to the boil. Once boiling, reduce the heat to medium and cook for 7–8 minutes until everything is tender and the stew has thickened.

5 Meanwhile, chop the tortillas into triangles and arrange them on a baking tray. Drizzle with olive oil and sprinkle with a pinch of salt. Bake for 4–5 minutes, or until crisp.

6 Once everything's ready, chop the lime in half. Squeeze half into the stew, then cut the remaining half into wedges. Serve the stew in bowls topped with the sliced avocado and reserved sliced onion. Scatter over the chopped coriander, then drizzle with some olive oil and season with black pepper. Serve with the lime wedges, for squeezing.

# Herby green shakshuka with butter beans and toasted ciabatta

| | |
|---|---|
| 1 | Leek |
| 2 | Garlic cloves |
| 1 tsp | Cumin seeds |
| 2 tbsp | Plant-based mayo |
| ½ tsp | Ground turmeric |
| ½ | Lemon |
| 400g tin | Butter beans |
| 1 | Vegetable stock cube |
| 2 | Ciabatta rolls |
| Handful | Dill |
| Handful | Coriander |
| Handful | Baby spinach |
| ½ tsp | Chilli flakes |
| 2 tbsp | Crispy dried onions |

1 Preheat the oven to 220°C/200°C fan/gas mark 7.

2 Top, tail and finely slice the leek. Slice the garlic. Heat a drizzle of olive oil in a large, deep-sided frying pan over a medium heat. Add the leek, garlic and cumin seeds and cook for 3–4 minutes.

3 Meanwhile, add 1 tablespoon of the mayo to a small bowl with the turmeric and a pinch of salt. Cut the lemon half in two and squeeze in one of the quarters. Mix to combine and set aside for later.

4 Add the butter beans (no need to drain) to the leek pan, and crumble in the stock cube. Bring to the boil, then reduce the heat to low and simmer for 3–4 minutes.

5 Meanwhile, put the ciabatta rolls into the oven for 3–4 minutes until warm and crusty. Strip the dill and coriander leaves from their stalks. Set aside some of the leaves for garnish, then finely chop the rest.

6 Stir the spinach, chopped herbs and remaining mayo into the pan of beans, along with a small splash of water, and cook for 1 minute or until the spinach has wilted. Squeeze in the remaining lemon juice and season with plenty of pepper.

7 Serve the herby green shakshuka drizzled with the turmeric mayo. Garnish with the chilli flakes, reserved coriander and dill leaves and crispy onions. Drizzle with some olive oil and season witha pinch of pepper. Serve the warm ciabatta on the side for dipping.

20 mins
Serves 2

# Spicy tofu larb lettuce cups with fresh herbs, lime and basmati rice

| | |
|---|---|
| 150g | Basmati rice |
| 2 | Garlic cloves |
| 30g | Fresh ginger |
| 1 | Red chilli |
| 1 | Shallot |
| 280g | Firm tofu |
| Handful | Mint |
| Handful | Coriander |
| 2 | Little gem lettuces |
| 1 tsp | Sriracha |
| 1 tbsp | Soy sauce |
| 1 tsp | Caster sugar |
| 1 | Lime |

1   In a sieve, rinse the rice with cold water, then tip into a saucepan and cover with 300ml boiling water. Cover with a lid and place over a high heat. Bring to the boil, then reduce the heat to a low simmer and leave to cook for 10–12 minutes. Once all the water has evaporated, take off the heat and set aside.

2   Meanwhile, peel and finely chop the garlic and ginger. Finely chop the red chilli. Finely slice the shallot. Drain the tofu and pat it dry with kitchen paper. Pick the mint leaves from the stalks and finely chop the leaves. Finely chop the coriander, including the stalks. Trim the roots from the little gem lettuces and separate the leaves.

3   Heat a drizzle of vegetable oil in a large, deep-sided frying pan over a medium–high heat. Once hot, crumble the tofu into the pan in small mince-like pieces. Cook for 4–5 minutes until starting to crisp and colour, then add the chopped garlic, ginger and chilli and cook for 2 minutes more.

4   Add the sriracha, soy sauce and sugar, then squeeze in the lime juice. Cook for a final 1–2 minutes, then remove the pan from the heat. Stir through the chopped herbs and sliced shallot.

5   Fill each of your lettuce cups with some rice and a spoonful of spicy tofu larb.

# Lemony pesto orzo stew with courgette, cherry tomatoes and fresh basil

| | |
|---|---|
| 1 | Leek |
| 3 | Garlic cloves |
| 200g | Orzo |
| ½ tsp | Chilli flakes |
| 2 | Vegetable stock cubes |
| 1 | Courgette |
| 250g | Cherry tomatoes |
| Handful | Basil |
| 100g | Plant-based green pesto |
| 1 tbsp | Nutritional yeast |
| Handful | Baby spinach |
| 1 | Lemon |

1 Top, tail and finely slice the leek. Heat a drizzle of olive oil in a large, deep-sided pan over a medium heat. Add the sliced leek, along with a pinch of salt, and cook for 3 minutes until starting to soften.

2 Peel and crush the garlic, then add to the pan, along with the orzo and half the chilli flakes. Cook for 1 minute, then crumble in the veg stock cubes and pour in 800ml boiling water. Stir and simmer for 6 minutes or until the orzo is nearly tender.

3 Meanwhile, halve the courgette lengthways. Peel one half into ribbons, then stack the ribbons and halve them lengthways. Add the courgette ribbons to a medium bowl and set aside, then slice the remaining courgette into half-moons. Chop the cherry tomatoes in half and finely chop the basil. Once the orzo is almost cooked, add the tomatoes and sliced courgette and cook for 2 minutes, then add the pesto, nutritional yeast and spinach, and stir until the spinach is wilted.

4 Squeeze the lemon and use a quarter of the juice to dress the courgette ribbons, along with a drizzle of olive oil and a pinch of salt. Stir the remaining lemon juice into the orzo, along with the chopped basil, and season to taste.

5 Serve the lemony pesto orzo stew in bowls, each topped with a bundle of courgette ribbons. Garnish with the remaining chilli flakes and season with a pinch of pepper.

# Miso aubergine and sticky coconut rice with steamed kale and avocado

30 mins
Serves 2

| | |
|---|---|
| 1 | Aubergine |
| 150g | Basmati rice |
| 50g | Coconut cream |
| 2 tbsp | Miso paste |
| 1 tbsp | Soy sauce |
| 1 | Avocado |
| 1 | Lime |
| 2 | Spring onions |
| 1 | Red chilli |
| 200g | Kale |
| 1 tsp | Sesame seeds |

1 Preheat the oven to 220°C/200°C fan/gas mark 7.

2 Halve the aubergine lengthways and score the flesh in a criss-cross pattern with a sharp knife, scoring about 1cm deep. Place the aubergine halves on a baking tray and drizzle with vegetable oil. Roast for 20 minutes.

3 Meanwhile, rinse the rice in a sieve, then tip into a saucepan and add 350ml boiling water. Crumble in the coconut cream. Place the pan over a medium heat and simmer with the lid on for 15–17 minutes until most of the water has been absorbed and the rice is soft and sticky. Set aside with the lid still on.

4 In a small bowl, combine the miso paste and soy sauce with a drizzle of vegetable oil and 1–2 tablespoons water. Mix well. Once the aubergine halves have been in the oven for 20 minutes, remove and spoon this miso mixture over the top. Return to the oven for a final 10 minutes until soft and jammy.

5 Peel, stone and slice the avocado and squeeze over half the lime juice. Thinly slice the spring onions and red chilli and set aside. Roughly chop the kale and add to a saucepan over a high heat with 200ml boiling water and a pinch of salt. Cover and lightly steam for 3–4 minutes until softened, then drain well. At the same time, toast the sesame seeds in a dry frying pan over a high heat for 2 minutes until golden.

6 When everything is ready, serve the aubergine and rice alongside the steamed kale and sliced avocado. Scatter over the sesame seeds, sliced red chilli and spring onions, and finish with a good squeeze of the remaining lime.

# Onion bhaji wraps with coriander chutney and chilli mayo

| | |
|---|---|
| 1 | Onion |
| 1 | Carrot |
| 1 | Courgette |
| Handful | Coriander |
| 2 tsp | Medium curry powder |
| 1 tsp | Ground fenugreek |
| 100g | Gram flour |
| 1 | Spring onion |
| Handful | Coriander |
| 1 | Lime |
| 1 tbsp | Plant-based mayo |
| 1 tsp | Chilli jam |
| 4 | Flatbreads or wraps |
| 1 | Little gem lettuce |
| 1 | Red chilli |
| 1 tsp | Nigella seeds |

1 Finely slice the onion, peel and grate the carrot and courgette, and chop the coriander. Put it all into a large bowl, along with the curry powder, fenugreek, gram flour and a pinch of salt and pepper. Measure 200ml cold water and slowly add to the bowl, stirring as you pour, until the mixture forms a thick batter. Set aside.

2 To make the coriander chutney, roughly chop the spring onion, then add to a blender with the coriander and 2 tablespoons of vegetable oil. Squeeze in the lime juice and season with salt, then blitz until smooth. In a separate bowl, mix together the mayo and chilli jam.

3 Heat a generous drizzle of vegetable oil in a large frying pan over a medium–high heat. Carefully add golf ball-sized spoonfuls of the bhaji mixture to the pan, pressing each one down a little, and cook for 3–4 minutes on each side until golden and crisp (you will need to do this in batches).

4 When all the bhajis are ready, heat the flatbreads in a separate dry pan over a medium–high heat for 1–2 minutes until nicely toasted. Shred the little gem lettuce. Finely slice the red chilli.

5 Top each flatbread with some lettuce, a few bhajis and a drizzle of both the chilli jam mayo and the coriander chutney. Finish with some red chilli slices, a pinch of the nigella seeds, then wrap and serve.

30 mins
Serves 2

# Harissa sweet potato lentil stew with balsamic dressing, crispy kale and avocado

| | |
|---|---|
| 1 | Sweet potato |
| 1 | Red pepper |
| 1 | Red onion |
| 250g | Cherry tomatoes |
| 2 tbsp | Rose harissa |
| 400g tin | Lentils |
| Handful | Parsley |
| 200g | Kale |
| 1 | Avocado |
| 1 tbsp | Balsamic vinegar |

1 Preheat the oven to 220°C/200°C fan/gas mark 7.

2 Chop the sweet potato into 2cm cubes and slice the red pepper into 1cm strips. Toss on a baking tray with a drizzle of vegetable oil and a pinch of salt and pepper. Roast for 15–20 minutes until cooked through.

3 Meanwhile, finely dice the red onion and halve the cherry tomatoes. Heat a drizzle of vegetable oil in a frying pan over a medium heat. Add the red onion and fry for 5–6 minutes until soft, then add the tomatoes, harissa paste and lentils (no need to drain). Bring to the boil, then reduce the heat to low and simmer for 4–5 minutes. Roughly chop the parsley and stir it through the stew.

4 Meanwhile, roughly chop the kale, then spread it out on a second baking tray. Drizzle with oil and season with a pinch of salt. Roast for 4–5 minutes until turning crispy, then remove from the oven and set aside.

5 Peel, stone and finely slice the avocado, then set aside. Remove the roasted sweet potato and red pepper from the oven and add to the lentil pan. Gently stir to combine (off the heat). In a small bowl, mix the balsamic vinegar with 2 tablespoons olive oil. Spoon the stew into shallow bowls and top with the crispy kale and avocado. Drizzle over the balsamic dressing and serve.

# Creamy mushroom and butter bean stroganoff with roasted carrot, parsnip and pumpkin seeds

| | |
|---|---|
| 1 | Parsnip |
| 1 | Carrot |
| 1 | Onion |
| 3 | Garlic cloves |
| 4 | Portobello mushrooms |
| 1 tbsp | Smoked paprika |
| 1 tsp | Dijon mustard |
| 400g tin | Butter beans |
| 1 | Vegetable stock cube |
| 1 tbsp | Nutritional yeast |
| 200ml | Coconut milk |
| Handful | Parsley |
| 1 | Lemon |
| 20g | Pumpkin seeds |

1   Preheat the oven to 220°C/200°C fan/gas mark 7.

2   Halve the parsnip and carrot lengthways (don't peel), and then slice into thick wedges. Toss on a baking tray with a drizzle of olive oil and a pinch of salt. Roast for 25–30 minutes until golden.

3   Meanwhile, finely slice the onion and garlic. Roughly slice the mushrooms. Heat a drizzle of olive oil in a large, deep-sided pan over a medium heat. Add the onion and fry for 4–5 minutes, then add the garlic, smoked paprika and Dijon mustard. Stir for a further minute before adding the mushrooms, then cook for another 4–5 minutes. Add the butter beans to the pan (no need to drain). Crumble in the stock cube, and stir in the nutritional yeast, coconut milk and 100ml boiling water. Bring to the boil, then reduce the heat to low and simmer for 8–10 minutes to thicken.

4   Roughly chop the parsley and add half of it to the pan. Squeeze in half of the lemon juice and cook for a further 2 minutes, then season to taste with salt and pepper.

5   Add the pumpkin seeds to the baking tray with the carrots and parsnips for the final few minutes to toast. Once the veg is cooked, remove from the oven.

6   To serve, divide the stroganoff into shallow bowls and top with the remaining parsley and the toasted pumpkin seeds. Serve the roasted veg alongside, finished with a squeeze of lemon.

# Miso mushrooms and pickled slaw with wedges and spicy guacamole

| | |
|---|---|
| 2 | Potatoes |
| 1 | Carrot |
| 1 | Cucumber |
| 2 | Spring onions |
| 1 tbsp | Sesame oil |
| 1 tbsp | Rice vinegar |
| 4 | Portobello mushrooms |
| 30g | Fresh ginger |
| 1 tbsp | Miso paste |
| 1 tsp | Caster sugar |
| 1 tsp | Sesame seeds |
| 1 | Avocado |
| 1 | Red chilli |
| 1 | Lime |

1 Preheat the oven to 220°C/200°C fan/gas mark 7.

2 Chop the potatoes into medium wedges, and toss on a baking tray with a drizzle of vegetable oil and a pinch of salt and pepper. Roast for 20–25 minutes until golden brown, turning them halfway through.

3 Meanwhile, prepare the slaw. Peel the carrot, then halve it lengthways and finely slice. Halve the cucumber lengthways, scoop out the seeds and finely slice, then finely chop the spring onions. Place it all in a large bowl with the sesame oil and the rice vinegar, and mix well. Set aside to lightly pickle.

4 Arrange the mushrooms gills down on a separate baking tray and roast for 10 minutes. Meanwhile, finely chop half the ginger. In a small bowl, mix the miso paste with the chopped ginger, the sugar, 1 tablespoon water and a drizzle of vegetable oil. Remove the mushrooms from the oven and turn over, then spoon over the miso sauce. Return to the hot oven for a further 5 minutes until soft and juicy.

5 Toast the sesame seeds in a dry pan over a high heat for 2 minutes until golden, then set aside. To make the spicy guacamole, peel, stone and mash the avocado, finely grate the remaining ginger, and finely chop half the red chilli. Mix these together in a bowl, then squeeze in the lime and season with a pinch of salt.

6 Finely slice the remaining red chilli. Once the wedges and mushrooms are cooked, remove from the oven and serve alongside the pickled slaw and guacamole, with the sesame seeds and sliced red chilli scattered over the top.

# Mediterranean vegetable risotto with toasted pumpkin seeds and fresh basil

| | |
|---|---|
| 1 | Aubergine |
| 1 | Red pepper |
| 1 | Courgette |
| 1 | Red onion |
| 2 | Garlic cloves |
| 150g | Arborio rice |
| 50ml | White wine |
| 2 tbsp | Sun-dried tomato purée |
| 1 | Vegetable stock cube |
| 1 tbsp | Nutritional yeast |
| Handful | Basil |
| 20g | Pumpkin seeds |

1   Preheat the oven to 220°C/200°C fan/gas mark 7.

2   Chop the aubergine, red pepper and courgette into small 2cm chunks and place them in a large roasting tray with a drizzle of olive oil, and a pinch of salt and pepper. Mix everything together and roast for 20 minutes until the vegetables are golden brown and lightly charred.

3   Meanwhile, finely dice the red onion and garlic. Heat a drizzle of olive oil in a large, deep-sided frying pan over a medium heat. Add the onion and garlic, along with a pinch of salt, and fry for 5 minutes until soft. Add the rice and white wine and cook for a further minute, stirring continually to stop the rice from sticking. Mix in the sun-dried tomato purée and reduce the heat to low.

4   Crumble the stock cube into a large jug and pour in 800ml boiling water. Stir well, then gradually add the stock to the pan, adding about 100ml at a time and letting each addition absorb into the rice before you add more. This should take a few minutes, then gently simmer 20–25 minutes. Once all the liquid is absorbed and the rice is cooked, stir through the nutritional yeast. Finely chop the basil and add this too.

5   When the roasted vegetables have 2 minutes of roasting time left, add the pumpkin seeds to the tray to toast, then remove the roasted vegetables from the oven and stir half of them into the risotto. Divide the risotto between two plates and spoon over the remaining roasted vegetables and the toasted pumpkin seeds to serve.

# New potato, broccoli and lentil traybake with walnut, garlic and herb dressing

| | |
|---|---|
| 500g | New potatoes |
| 150g | Radishes |
| 1 | Onion |
| 1 | Red pepper |
| 1 tsp | Dried oregano |
| 2 | Garlic cloves |
| Handful | Parsley |
| 30g | Walnuts |
| 1 | Lemon |
| 1 tbsp | Balsamic vinegar |
| 200g | Tenderstem broccoli |
| 200g | Pre-cooked Beluga lentils pouch |

1   Preheat the oven to 220°C/200°C fan/gas mark 7.

2   Roughly chop the new potatoes into 1cm slices and place in a saucepan of boiling water. Parboil for 4–5 minutes, then drain.

3   Meanwhile, trim the stalks off the radishes and cut them in half, cut the onion into wedges and slice the red pepper into thin strips. Combine these vegetables on a baking tray. Drizzle with olive oil, sprinkle over the oregano and season with a pinch of salt and pepper. Add the drained new potatoes to the same tray and toss together. Place in the oven for an initial 20 minutes.

4   To make the dressing, crush the garlic and finely chop the parsley and walnuts. Cut the lemon in half. In a small bowl, combine the balsamic vinegar with 2 tablespoons olive oil and a pinch of salt and pepper. Add the garlic, parsley and walnuts, and squeeze in half the lemon. Mix and set aside for later.

5   Once the veg has been roasting for 20 minutes, remove the tray from the oven and add the broccoli and lentils. Return to the oven for another 15 minutes, or until everything is golden and crisp. Once it's ready, remove from the oven and pour over the dressing. Mix and serve with a good squeeze of the remaining lemon.

# Sticky tofu rice noodle salad with chilli and mirin dressing

| | |
|---|---|
| 2 | Garlic cloves |
| 2 tbsp | Soy sauce |
| ½ tsp | Chilli flakes |
| 1 tsp | Mirin |
| 1 tsp | Caster sugar |
| 200g | Flat rice noodles |
| 280g | Firm tofu |
| 3 tbsp | Cornflour |
| 1 | Carrot |
| Handful | Radishes |
| 2 | Spring onions |
| 1 tbsp | Agave syrup |
| 1 tsp | Sesame seeds |

1   Crush the garlic and add it to a bowl with 1 tablespoon of the soy sauce, and the chilli flakes, mirin and sugar. Mix well and set aside. This is your dressing.

2   Bring a saucepan of water to the boil and add the rice noodles. Stir well for a minute, then remove from the heat and leave to soak for 8–10 minutes until cooked through.

3   Drain and pat dry the tofu with kitchen paper, then cut it into 1cm thick triangles. Add the tofu to a large bowl with the remaining soy sauce and mix until all the soy sauce has been absorbed. Sprinkle the cornflour over the tofu and toss together until fully coated. Peel and grate the carrot and finely slice the radishes into a separate large bowl, and mix well. Roughly slice the spring onions and set aside.

4   Heat a generous drizzle of vegetable oil in a frying pan over a medium–high heat. Once hot, add the coated tofu and cook for 7–8 minutes, turning regularly until golden and crisp. Add the agave syrup and sesame seeds to the pan for the final minute, and stir to coat the tofu well. Once done, transfer to a plate and set aside. Wipe the pan clean.

5   Once the noodles are cooked through, drain well and add to the frying pan, along with the dressing. Cook over a medium heat for 1–2 minutes until the dressing has coated the noodles. Remove from the pan and mix through the bowl of veg.

6   Serve the rice noodles alongside the sticky tofu pieces, topped with the spring onions.

# Juicy harissa mushroom shawarma with cucumber, dill bulgur and pickled onions

45 mins
Serves 2

| | |
|---|---|
| 1 | Red onion |
| 80g | Bulgur wheat |
| 1 | Vegetable stock cube |
| 4 | Garlic cloves |
| 1 tbsp | Rose harissa |
| 1 tsp | Dried oregano |
| 1 tsp | Ground cumin |
| 6 | Portobello mushrooms |
| 1 tsp | Caster sugar |
| 1 | Lemon |
| 2 tbsp | Plant-based mayo |
| 1 | Cucumber |
| Handful | Dill |
| 4 | Wooden skewers, soaked in water |

1. Dice half the red onion, then heat a drizzle of olive oil in a saucepan over a medium heat. Add the diced onion and soften for 3–4 minutes. In a sieve, rinse the bulgur wheat under cold water, then add to the pan. Crumble in the stock cube and pour in 180ml boiling water. Bring to the boil, then cover and reduce the heat to low. Simmer for 15 minutes. Once done, transfer to a bowl, stir and set aside to cool.

2. Crush 2 of the garlic cloves into a bowl and add the harissa, oregano, cumin and 2 tablespoons olive oil. Season with salt and pepper. Roughly chop the mushrooms and add them to the bowl. Stir and set aside to marinate. Preheat the grill to high.

3. For the pickle, finely slice the remaining onion half and add it to a bowl. Add a pinch of salt and the sugar, then squeeze over half the lemon. Pour over enough boiling water to cover, then set aside to pickle.

4. Crush the remaining garlic into a separate bowl and mix with the mayo and 1 teaspoon cold water. Set aside.

5. Skewer the mushrooms and arrange them on a baking tray lined with baking paper. Grill for 15 minutes, turning once halfway through cooking.

6. Top and tail the cucumber, then halve lengthways. Deseed and finely dice. Finely chop the dill. Stir the cucumber, dill and remaining lemon juice through the bulgur wheat.

7. Drain the pickled onions. Serve the mushroom shawarma over the bulgur and top with the pickled onions. Serve with the garlic mayo on the side for dipping.

# Coronation chickpea and sticky cashew salad with fresh chilli and spring onions

| | |
|---|---|
| 30g | Cashews |
| 2 tbsp | Mango chutney |
| 400g tin | Chickpeas |
| 2 tsp | Mild curry powder |
| 1 tbsp | Plant-based mayo |
| ½ tsp | Ground turmeric |
| 40g | Dried apricots |
| 1 | Lemon |
| 2 | Little gem lettuces |
| Handful | Coriander |
| 1 | Red chilli |
| 2 | Spring onions |
| 1 tsp | Nigella seeds |

1   Toast the cashews in dry frying over a medium–high heat for 3–4 minutes, then add half the mango chutney and cook for 1 minute further until coated and sticky. Set aside in a bowl.

2   Return the pan to a medium heat and add a drizzle of olive oil. Drain the chickpeas and add them to the pan, along with half the curry powder. Cook for 3–4 minutes until warmed through.

3   To make the coronation sauce, mix together the mayo and turmeric in a large bowl. Chop the apricots and stir them in, along with the remaining curry powder and remaining mango chutney. Cut the lemon in two and squeeze one half into this mixture, then season with salt. Once the chickpeas are warmed through, add them to the bowl and mix well.

4   Trim the roots from the little gem lettuces and roughly tear the bigger leaves. Finely shred the inner cores. Pick the coriander leaves from their stalks. Finely slice the red chilli and spring onion, and cut the remaining lemon half into wedges.

5   To serve, divide the lettuce between bowls and spoon over the coronation chickpeas. Sprinkle with the coriander leaves, nigella seeds and sticky cashews. Garnish with the red chilli and spring onion, and serve with the lemon wedges for squeezing.

# Miso-roasted squash with dill and tahini yoghurt and pomegranate molasses

| | |
|---|---|
| 1 | Butternut squash |
| 1 | Red onion |
| 1 tbsp | Tahini |
| Handful | Dill |
| 2 tbsp | Coconut yoghurt |
| 2 | Garlic cloves |
| 1 tbsp | Pomegranate molasses |
| 200g | Tenderstem broccoli |
| 1 tbsp | Miso paste |
| 1 tbsp | Za'atar |

1 Preheat the oven to 220°C/200°C fan/gas mark 7.

2 Cut the squash in half, remove any seeds, and chop the flesh into 1cm-thick slices. Arrange on a large baking tray. Cut the onion into thick wedges and add to the tray. Drizzle with a generous amount of olive oil, season with a good pinch of salt and pepper, and roast in the oven for an initial 10–15 minutes.

3 Meanwhile, in a small bowl, mix the tahini with 2–3 tablespoon cold water until the mixture runs smoothly off a spoon. Finely chop half the dill and stir this in, along with the coconut yoghurt. Set aside.

4 Crush the garlic and add it to a second bowl, along with the pomegranate molasses and a good drizzle of olive oil. Season with salt and pepper, and mix well.

5 Remove the squash from the oven and add the Tenderstem broccoli and miso paste to the tray. Mix well to coat the vegetables in the miso paste before returning to the oven for another 10 minutes until the squash is golden brown and cooked through.

6 Once the vegetables have finished cooking, sprinkle over the za'atar and mix well. Spoon the yoghurt on to plates and top with the miso-roasted vegetables. Finish with spoonfuls of the pomegranate dressing and the remaining dill torn over the top.

# Korean tempeh and grain lettuce tacos with spicy peanut sauce and carrot slaw

| | |
|---|---|
| 280g | Tempeh |
| 1 tbsp | Soy sauce |
| 2 | Little gem lettuces |
| 1 | Carrot |
| Handful | Mint |
| Handful | Coriander |
| 30g | Peanuts |
| 1 | Lime |
| 2 tbsp | Sesame oil |
| 1 tbsp | Agave syrup |
| 1 tbsp | Miso paste |
| 2 tbsp | Smooth peanut butter |
| 1 tbsp | Sriracha |
| 250g | Pre-cooked mixed grain pouch |

1   Cut the tempeh into 1cm slices. Add to a large bowl and mix with the soy sauce and a drizzle of vegetable oil. Leave to marinate while you prepare everything else.

2   Remove 1cm of the root from the little gem lettuces and separate the outer leaves; these will be your taco cups. Thinly slice the remaining leaves. Peel and grate the carrot, then chop the mint and coriander, and roughly chop the peanuts. Zest and juice the lime.

3   Add the sliced lettuce, carrot, mint and coriander to a bowl, along with half the lime juice and all of its grated zest, half the chopped peanuts and half the sesame oil. Toss to combine and season with a pinch of salt and pepper. Set aside.

4   To make the sauce, whisk the remaining lime juice and sesame oil in a small bowl, then add the agave syrup, miso paste, peanut butter and sriracha and whisk again. Loosen with cold water if needed.

5   Heat a drizzle of vegetable oil in a frying pan over a medium heat. Add the tempeh and fry for 3–4 minutes on each side until golden. Heat the pre-cooked grains as per the packet instructions.

6   To serve, spoon the pre-cooked grains into the lettuce cups, followed by the carrot slaw. Top with the tempeh, then drizzle over the peanut dressing and finish with the remaining peanuts.

# Thai quinoa rainbow salad with spicy peanut dressing

| | |
|---|---|
| 80g | Quinoa |
| 1 | Vegetable stock cube |
| 1 | Cucumber |
| ½ | Red cabbage |
| 1 | Red pepper |
| 2 | Spring onions |
| 1 | Carrot |
| 1 tbsp | Sesame oil |
| 1 tbsp | Agave syrup |
| 1 tbsp | Miso paste |
| 2 tbsp | Peanut butter |
| 1 tbsp | Sriracha |
| 1 | Lime |
| Handful | Unsalted peanuts |

1 Add the quinoa to a saucepan and cover with 500ml boiling water. Crumble in the stock cube. Bring to the boil, lid on, then reduce the heat to a low simmer and cook for 20–25 minutes until the quinoa is soft. Drain and set aside.

2 Cut the cucumber in half lengthways, thinly slice and place into a large bowl. Finely chop the red cabbage, finely dice the red pepper and slice the spring onions. Peel and finely chop the carrot, and add everything to the bowl with the cucumber.

3 To make the dressing, combine the sesame oil, agave syrup, miso paste, peanut butter and sriracha in a bowl. Squeeze in the lime, then mix well. Add a touch of water if you need to loosen it; it should be the consistency of thick cream. Set aside.

4 Roughly chop the peanuts. To serve, add the cooked quinoa to the bowl of chopped vegetables and pour the dressing over the top. Serve topped with the crushed peanuts.

# Crispy butter bean, tomato, kale and pesto traybake with garlic ciabatta

| | |
|---|---|
| 400g tin | Butter beans |
| 1 | Red onion |
| 250g | Cherry tomatoes |
| 4 | Garlic cloves |
| 2 tbsp | Sun-dried tomato purée |
| 1 tbsp | Balsamic vinegar |
| 2 | Ciabatta rolls |
| Handful | Kale |
| 2 tbsp | Plant-based green pesto |
| 1 | Lemon |
| Handful | Basil |

1 Preheat the oven to 220°C/200°C fan/gas mark 7.

2 Drain and rinse the butter beans and tip into a baking tray. Chop the red onion into wedges and add to the tray, along with the cherry tomatoes (whole). Drizzle with olive oil and season with salt and pepper. Roast for an initial 5 minutes.

3 Meanwhile, crush 2 of the garlic cloves and add to a small bowl, along with the sun-dried tomato purée and balsamic vinegar. Season with salt and pepper, and add a drizzle of olive oil. Mix well. Remove the veg from the oven and pour this mixture over the top, then mix through before returning to the oven for a further 8 minutes.

4 Slice the ciabatta rolls in half and place on a second baking tray. Crush the remaining garlic and add to a small bowl with a drizzle of olive oil. Mix well, then spread evenly on to the rolls. Remove the thick stalks from the kale and roughly chop the leaves. Add to the oven tray full of veg with a drizzle of olive oil and a pinch of salt and pepper for a final 5 minutes until crispy. Add the ciabatta tray to the oven for the same time.

5 Once the veg is cooked, remove from the oven. Finish with dollops of the green pesto and a good squeeze of lemon juice. Tear over the basil leaves and serve alongside the garlicky ciabatta rolls.

# Roasted radish, fresh orange and Tenderstem poke bowl with sriracha mayo

| | |
|---|---|
| 150g | Basmati rice |
| 250g | Radishes |
| 1 tbsp | Sesame oil |
| 2 tbsp | Soy sauce |
| 1 tsp | Caster sugar |
| 1 | Cucumber |
| 1 tbsp | Mirin |
| 1 | Avocado |
| 1 tbsp | Plant-based mayo |
| 1 tsp | Sriracha |
| 200g | Tenderstem broccoli |
| 1 large | Orange |
| 2 tsp | Sesame seeds |

1 Preheat the oven to 220°C/200°C fan/gas mark 7 and line a baking tray with baking paper.

2 In a sieve, rinse the rice with cold water, then tip into a saucepan and cover with 300ml boiling water. Cover and bring to the boil over a high heat, then reduce the heat to low and simmer for 10–12 minutes. Once all the water has evaporated, take off the heat and set aside.

3 Trim the stalks off the radishes and chop them into quarters. Add the chopped radishes to one side of the prepared tray. Drizzle with the sesame oil and 1 tablespoon of the soy sauce. Scatter over the sugar, then mix together and roast for an initial 10 minutes.

4 Meanwhile, finely slice the cucumber and add it to a medium bowl with the mirin and a good pinch of salt. Mix and set aside to pickle. Peel, stone and finely slice the avocado. Combine the mayo with the sriracha in a small bowl and loosen with a little water for a drizzly consistency.

5 After 10 minutes, remove the tray from the oven and add the Tenderstem broccoli to the other side. Cut the orange in half and squeeze one half over the broccoli, then drizzle with the remaining 1 tablespoon soy sauce. Return the tray to the oven for 10 minutes more until everything is golden and tender.

6 Trim the skin off the remaining orange and roughly chop into chunks. Assemble your poke bowls with the rice, cucumber, avocado, orange chunks and roasted broccoli and radishes. Garnish the radishes and avocado with sesame seeds and drizzle over the sriracha mayo to serve.

# Spring green pesto risotto with homemade cashew, basil and miso pesto

| | |
|---|---|
| 1 | Onion |
| 4 | Garlic cloves |
| 2 | Vegetable stock cubes |
| 150g | Arborio rice |
| 100ml | White wine |
| 30g | Cashews |
| Handful | Basil |
| Handful | Rocket |
| 1 tbsp | Miso paste |
| 1 tbsp | Nutritional yeast |
| 1 | Lemon |
| 1 | Courgette |
| 200g | Sugar snap peas |
| 2 | Spring onions |

1   Dice the onion and crush 2 of the garlic cloves. Heat a drizzle of olive oil in a large, deep-sided frying pan over a medium heat. Add the onion and garlic, along with a pinch of salt, and cook for 4–5 minutes until softened. In a jug, dissolve the stock cubes in 800ml boiling water.

2   Once the onion has softened, add the rice and cook for 1 minute, then add the white wine and continue cooking for 1–2 minutes, stirring continually. Gradually add the stock to the pan, adding about 100ml at a time and letting each addition absorb into the rice before you add more, until the rice is cooked through and all the liquid is absorbed. This should take 20–25 minutes.

3   Meanwhile, add the cashews, basil, rocket, miso paste and nutritional yeast to a blender. Peel and add the remaining garlic, along with 4 tablespoons olive oil and a good pinch of salt. Squeeze in half the lemon and blitz until smooth.

4   Dice the courgette, and finely slice the sugar snaps and spring onions. Once the rice is almost done, add the courgette and sugar snaps to the pan and cook for 2 minutes until bright green but still crunchy. Remove the pan from the heat and stir through the pesto. Taste for seasoning and add a pinch of salt if needed.

5   Serve the risotto in bowls, topped with the spring onion slices, a drizzle of olive oil and a crack of black pepper. Cut the remaining lemon half into wedges and use as a garnish.

# THREE:

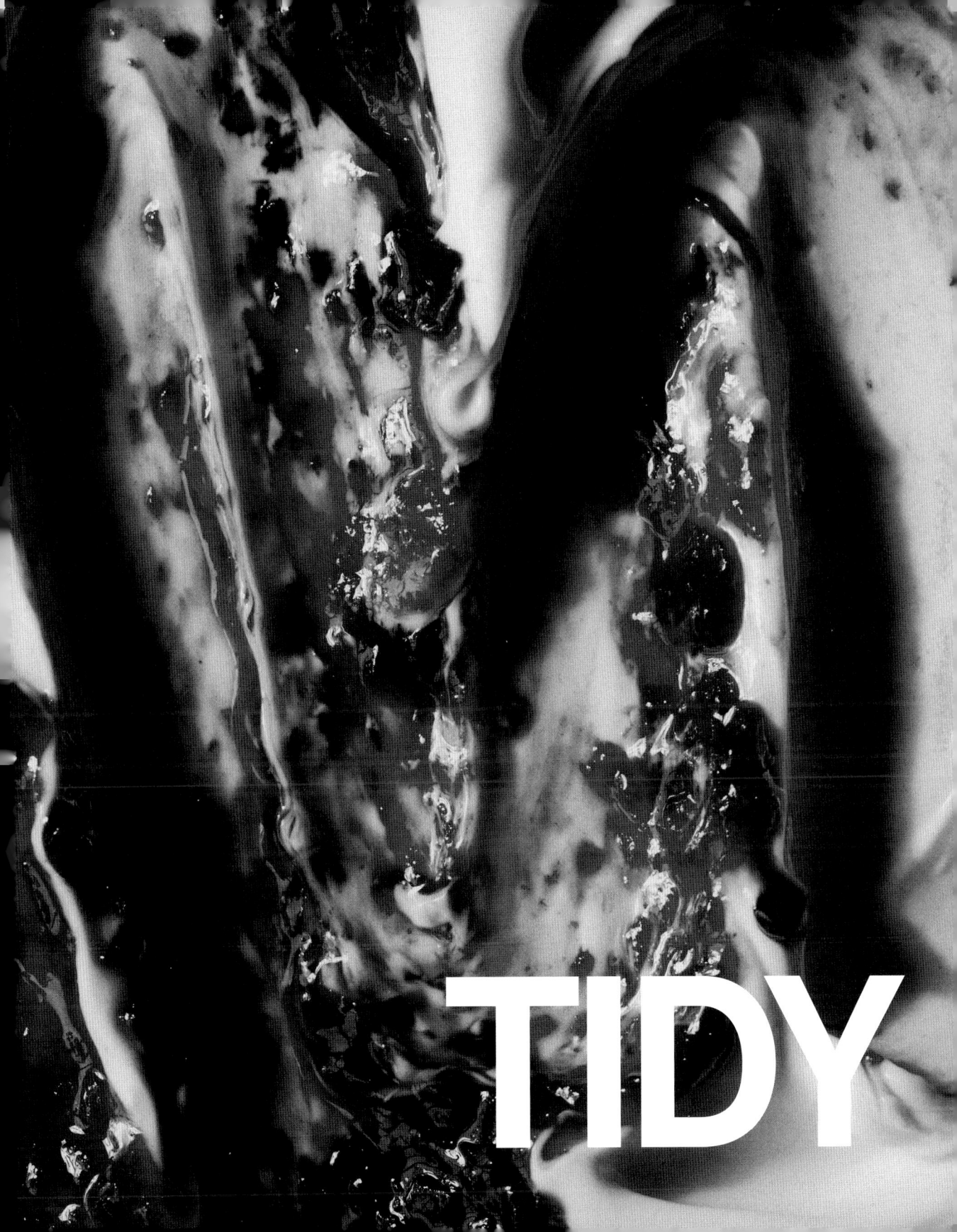

TIDY

# Three: Tidy

# Directory

# Comfort food

p44
○ Delicious
○ Not bad
○ Never again

Aubergine, lentil and courgette moussaka topped with creamy cashew béchamel sauce

p46
○ Delicious
○ Not bad
○ Never again

Cashew and avocado pesto pasta with griddled courgettes and sun-dried tomatoes

p48
○ Delicious
○ Not bad
○ Never again

Butternut squash risotto with crispy kale and toasted pumpkin seeds

p51
○ Delicious
○ Not bad
○ Never again

Cashew and mushroom spaghetti carbonara with fresh rocket

p53
○ Delicious
○ Not bad
○ Never again

Oven-baked chickpea dahl with chilli-cheese naans

p55
○ Delicious
○ Not bad
○ Never again

Creamy miso, coconut and aubergine ramen with udon noodles

p56
○ Delicious
○ Not bad
○ Never again

Crispy oyster mushroom burgers with pesto mayo and Parmentier potatoes

p59
○ Delicious
○ Not bad
○ Never again

Curried aubergine and fragrant rice with minty coconut yoghurt and beef tomato

p60
○ Delicious
○ Not bad
○ Never again

Chickpea, apricot and sweet potato tagine with herb and lemon bulgur wheat

p63
○ Delicious
○ Not bad
○ Never again

Sicilian aubergine linguine with sun-dried tomatoes, black olives and capers

p64 ○ Delicious ○ Not bad ○ Never again

Crispy pan-fried gnocchi bolognese with mushrooms and walnuts

p67 ○ Delicious ○ Not bad ○ Never again

Creamy rose harissa and butter bean stew with spinach, cherry tomatoes and fresh basil

p68 ○ Delicious ○ Not bad ○ Never again

Crispy gnocchi puttanesca with Tenderstem broccoli, roasted red onions and pumpkin seeds

p71 ○ Delicious ○ Not bad ○ Never again

Gochujang mac and 'cheese' with crispy sesame tofu

p72 ○ Delicious ○ Not bad ○ Never again

Mushroom gyros with cucumber raita, Greek salad and oregano fries

p75 ○ Delicious ○ Not bad ○ Never again

Wild mushroom and leek risotto

p76 ○ Delicious ○ Not bad ○ Never again

Sri Lankan-style butternut and aubergine curry

p79 ○ Delicious ○ Not bad ○ Never again

Shepherdless pie with rich mushrooms, lentils and creamy mash

p80 ○ Delicious ○ Not bad ○ Never again

Classic mushroom lasagne with dressed rocket

p83 ○ Delicious ○ Not bad ○ Never again

Four-bean chilli-loaded sweet potatoes topped with zingy guacamole and harissa mayo

# Fakeaway treats

p88
- ○ Delicious
- ○ Not bad
- ○ Never again

Crispy chilli and sesame tofu with aromatic green beans

p91
- ○ Delicious
- ○ Not bad
- ○ Never again

'Nduja and broccoli pizza-style crispy flatbreads

p92
- ○ Delicious
- ○ Not bad
- ○ Never again

Aubergine and green bean Thai curry topped with fresh lime, chilli and coriander

p95
- ○ Delicious
- ○ Not bad
- ○ Never again

Black bean enchiladas with 'cheesy' topping and guacamole

p96
- ○ Delicious
- ○ Not bad
- ○ Never again

Sticky tofu, cashew and pepper stir-fry with sesame seeds and basmati rice

p99
- ○ Delicious
- ○ Not bad
- ○ Never again

Spanish tortilla with roasted pepper salad and garlic-and-herb aioli

p100
- ○ Delicious
- ○ Not bad
- ○ Never again

Satay-glazed aubergine with spicy green bean, peanut and carrot salad

p103
- ○ Delicious
- ○ Not bad
- ○ Never again

Oyster mushroom 'calamari' with pan con tomate, rocket and garlic aioli

p104
- ○ Delicious
- ○ Not bad
- ○ Never again

Creamy cashew and sweet potato korma with basmati rice

p107
- ○ Delicious
- ○ Not bad
- ○ Never again

Crispy tofu bánh mì with pickled slaw, sriracha mayo and fries

p108
○ Delicious
○ Not bad
○ Never again

Mexican bean tostadas with zingy sweetcorn salsa

p111
○ Delicious
○ Not bad
○ Never again

Patatas bravas and tofu nuggets with garlic aioli, homemade tomato sauce and pan-fried little gems

p112
○ Delicious
○ Not bad
○ Never again

Sticky mango tofu skewers with sticky coconut rice and charred sweetcorn salsa

p115
○ Delicious
○ Not bad
○ Never again

Oyster mushroom birria tacos with ancho dipping sauce

p116
○ Delicious
○ Not bad
○ Never again

Chilli greens udon noodles with Tenderstem broccoli and pak choi

p119
○ Delicious
○ Not bad
○ Never again

Crispy tofu burger, carrot slaw and chips with homemade chicken shop gravy

p120
○ Delicious
○ Not bad
○ Never again

Butternut squash and pinto 'quesadillas' with avocado salsa and coconut-lime sauce

p123
○ Delicious
○ Not bad
○ Never again

Tofu tikka masala with brown rice

p124
○ Delicious
○ Not bad
○ Never again

Smoky pulled aubergine and black bean-loaded fries with green goddess sauce

p127
○ Delicious
○ Not bad
○ Never again

Sweet-and-sour tofu with umami mushroom rice

# Healthy eats

p132
- ○ Delicious
- ○ Not bad
- ○ Never again

Mexican black bean stew with fresh avocado and toasted flatbreads

p135
- ○ Delicious
- ○ Not bad
- ○ Never again

Herby green shakshuka with butter beans and toasted ciabatta

p136
- ○ Delicious
- ○ Not bad
- ○ Never again

Spicy tofu larb lettuce cups with fresh herbs, lime and basmati rice

p139
- ○ Delicious
- ○ Not bad
- ○ Never again

Lemony pesto orzo stew with courgette, cherry tomatoes and fresh basil

p140
- ○ Delicious
- ○ Not bad
- ○ Never again

Miso aubergine and sticky coconut rice with steamed kale and avocado

p143
- ○ Delicious
- ○ Not bad
- ○ Never again

Onion bhaji wraps with coriander chutney and chilli mayo

p144
- ○ Delicious
- ○ Not bad
- ○ Never again

Harissa sweet potato lentil stew with balsamic dressing, crispy kale and avocado

p147
- ○ Delicious
- ○ Not bad
- ○ Never again

Creamy mushroom and butter bean stroganoff with roasted carrot, parsnips and pumpkin seeds

p148
- ○ Delicious
- ○ Not bad
- ○ Never again

Miso mushrooms and pickled slaw with wedges and spicy guacamole

p151
- ○ Delicious
- ○ Not bad
- ○ Never again

Mediterranean vegetable risotto with toasted pumpkin seeds and fresh basil

p152
- ○ Delicious
- ○ Not bad
- ○ Never again

New potato, broccoli and lentil traybake with walnut, garlic and herb dressing

p155
- ○ Delicious
- ○ Not bad
- ○ Never again

Sticky tofu rice noodle salad with chilli and mirin dressing

p156
- ○ Delicious
- ○ Not bad
- ○ Never again

Juicy harissa mushroom shawarma with cucumber, dill bulgur and pickled onions

p159
- ○ Delicious
- ○ Not bad
- ○ Never again

Coronation chickpea and sticky cashew salad with fresh chilli and spring onions

p160
- ○ Delicious
- ○ Not bad
- ○ Never again

Miso-roasted squash with dill and tahini yoghurt and pomegranate molasses

p162
- ○ Delicious
- ○ Not bad
- ○ Never again

Korean tempeh and grain lettuce tacos with spicy peanut sauce and carrot slaw

p165
- ○ Delicious
- ○ Not bad
- ○ Never again

Thai quinoa rainbow salad with spicy peanut dressing

p167
- ○ Delicious
- ○ Not bad
- ○ Never again

Crispy butter bean, tomato, kale and pesto traybake with garlic ciabattas

p168
- ○ Delicious
- ○ Not bad
- ○ Never again

Roasted radish, fresh orange and Tenderstem poke bowl with sriracha mayo

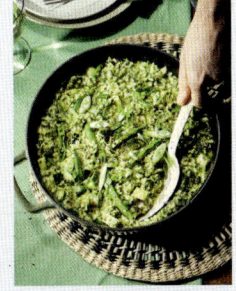

p171
- ○ Delicious
- ○ Not bad
- ○ Never again

Spring green pesto risotto with homemade cashew, basil and miso pesto

# Index

## Three: Tidy

# Thanks

The list of people to thank who've made Grubby happen is too long, but when I thought about it, the simplest way of describing those I'm most grateful to is everyone who took a punt on us in a variety of different ways.

Firstly, the team, many of which quit higher-paid jobs to join Grubby in the first place. They continue to make every day count with immense energy and positivity, all whilst having a laugh in the process, which has defined the Grubby culture. The suppliers and subcontractors who went out of their way to help us get started with little to no gain. Friends and family who volunteered to deliver flyers, knock doors and help pack during lockdown to get us our first customers. Our original angel investor who took a massive gamble on the idea and has been incredibly supportive ever since (plus all our other investors to boot!). Our photographer, stylist, and brand guys who make Grubby Grubby. My mum, dad and brother for countless honest chats, which have without doubt helped us avoid several potholes. And, lastly, the people who said it would never get off the ground and not to quit my job – I'm particularly grateful to them, they've been my fuel throughout.

This book though is for every single Grubby customer. You're the reason we exist, why we love what we do, and why we keep wanting to raise the bar. I can't wrap my head around how some of you have had a box virtually every single week since we launched. Even I haven't managed that. Legends.

Grubby turns five years old not long after this book goes on sale. The shocks, surprises, and stomach-churning highs and lows of the Grubby rollercoaster have been quite intense at times but we're still on the ride, strapped in, wanting more.

If you've read this far, thanks, but also stop reading and get cooking!

Martin Holden-White
Grubby Founder

1

Published in 2025 by Ebury Press,
an imprint of Ebury Publishing,
One Embassy Gardens, 8 Viaduct Gardens, London,
SW11 7BW

Ebury Press is part of the Penguin Random House
group of companies whose addresses can be found
at global.penguinrandomhouse.com

Penguin
Random House
UK

Text © Ebury Press
Photography © Uyen Luu
Design © Stephenson Edwards

Grubby Ltd. has asserted its right to be identified
as the author of this Work in accordance with the
Copyright, Designs and Patents Act 1988.

First published by Ebury Press in 2025.
www.penguin.co.uk

A CIP catalogue record for this book is available from
the British Library.

Author: Martin Holden-White
Recipes: Ferg Smithers and Hannah Mariaux
Photography: Uyen Luu
Food and prop styling: Lucy Rose Turnbull
Creative direction and design: Stephenson Edwards
Typesetting: Clare Sivell
Production: Percie Bridgwater
Project Editor: Fionn Hargreaves
Publishing Director: Elizabeth Bond

ISBN 9781529949735

Penguin Random House is committed to a sustainable
future for our business, our readers and our planet.
This book is made from Forest Stewardship Council®
certified paper.

MIX
Paper | Supporting
responsible forestry
FSC® C018179
FSC
www.fsc.org